T0279114

PRESENTED TO

_____

FROM

_____

DATE

_____

PRESENT
in
PRAYER

A GUIDED INVITATION TO PEACE
THROUGH BIBLICAL MEDITATION

JENNIFER TUCKER

THOMAS NELSON
Since 1798

Present in Prayer

Published in Nashville, Tennessee, by Thomas Nelson. Thomas Nelson is a registered trademark of HarperCollins Christian Publishing, Inc.

Thomas Nelson titles may be purchased in bulk for educational, business, fundraising, or sales promotional use. For information, please email SpecialMarkets@ThomasNelson.com.

Unless otherwise noted, Scripture quotations are taken from the Holy Bible, New Living Translation. © 1996, 2004, 2015 by Tyndale House Foundation. Used by permission of Tyndale House Ministries, Carol Stream, Illinois 60188. All rights reserved.

Scripture quotations marked CSB® are taken from the Christian Standard Bible®. Copyright © 2017 by Holman Bible Publishers. Used by permission. Christian Standard Bible® and CSB® are federally registered trademarks of Holman Bible Publishers.

Scripture quotations marked ESV are taken from the ESV® Bible (The Holy Bible, English Standard Version®). Copyright © 2001 by Crossway, a publishing ministry of Good News Publishers. Used by permission. All rights reserved.

Scripture quotations marked HCSB are taken from the Holman Christian Standard Bible®. Copyright © 1999, 2000, 2002, 2003, 2009 by Holman Bible Publishers. Used by permission. HCSB® is a federally registered trademark of Holman Bible Publishers.

Scripture quotations marked MSG are taken from THE MESSAGE. Copyright © 1993, 2002, 2018 by Eugene H. Peterson. Used by permission of NavPress. All rights reserved. Represented by Tyndale House Publishers, a Division of Tyndale House Ministries.

Scripture quotations marked NIV are taken from The Holy Bible, New International Version®, NIV®. Copyright © 1973, 1978, 1984, 2011 by Biblica, Inc.® Used by permission of Zondervan. All rights reserved worldwide. www.zondervan.com. The "NIV" and "New International Version" are trademarks registered in the United States Patent and Trademark Office by Biblica, Inc.®

Scripture quotations marked TLB are taken from The Living Bible. Copyright © 1971. Used by permission of Tyndale House Publishers, a Division of Tyndale House Ministries, Carol Stream, Illinois 60188. All rights reserved.

Any internet addresses, phone numbers, or company or product information printed in this book are offered as a resource and are not intended in any way to be or to imply an endorsement by Thomas Nelson, nor does Thomas Nelson vouch for the existence, content, or services of these sites, phone numbers, companies, or products beyond the life of this book.

Note to reader: The meditation and mindfulness practices provided in this book are offered as helpful tools to support and strengthen your mental and spiritual health. They are not magical, fix-all solutions, nor are they a replacement for medical treatment or professional therapy. If you are struggling with severe mental health symptoms that are interfering with your everyday life, please seek help from a trained and qualified professional.

Cover and interior art: Jennifer Tucker
Interior design: Jeff Jansen, Aesthetic Soup

ISBN 978-1-4002-4792-9 (HC)
ISBN 978-1-4002-4809-4 (audio)
ISBN 978-1-4002-4808-7 (eBook)

Printed in Malaysia

24 25 26 27 28 COS 5 4 3 2 1

To Mark,

my Velveteen love.

You're still the one.

CONTENTS

SEEDS AND SOULS

Cultivating a Deeply Rooted Life of Faith

*"Blessed are those who trust in the LORD and have
made the LORD their hope and confidence.
They are like trees planted along a riverbank,
with roots that reach deep into the water.
Such trees are not bothered by the heat or worried by long months of drought.
Their leaves stay green, and they never stop producing fruit."*
JEREMIAH 17:7–8

As a frantic and noisy world rushes by, quiet miracles are unfolding beneath the surface of things, in places unseen. This is where both seeds and souls begin to flourish.

Surrounded by silence, enveloped by the earth, tucked into the darkness of the soil, a seed is nourished and protected. In time, a shoot of life unfurls and reaches toward the surface while roots branch out and go down deep, deep, deeper into the quiet ground. While shoots and stalks, leaves and flowers, unfold in the light of the sun, what's happening beneath the surface is what makes growth possible. Roots anchor a growing plant in place, taking in water and food from the

fertile soil, storing nutrients, and transferring them to the rest of the plant, producing lovely blooms and life-giving fruit.

Without roots, a plant withers. Without roots, it cannot weather storms or drought. Without roots, there can be no fruit.

Our souls are seeds that require stillness and time so our roots can anchor deep in the fertile soil of God's Word. If we want our lives to produce fruit—particularly the lovely and life-giving fruit of the Spirit—our most important work begins in the silence, in the quiet and unseen places beneath the surface of our busy lives, shielded from the eyes of any audience and away from the noise of the world. It is here that we strengthen our roots, sinking them deep into the love of God and the truth of His Word.

If our roots are strong, the winds of worry won't uproot us, and the storms of anxiety won't wash us away. If we're deeply rooted, we may bend in the wind, but we won't break easily. When seasons and circumstances change, bringing droughts of discouragement or floods of suffering with them, we can remain anchored and secure, weathering any storm that might come.

Cultivating a life that flourishes with the fruit of the Spirit takes time and commitment and patience. Roots don't grow strong overnight. You can't hurry growth, and you can't rush spiritual formation.

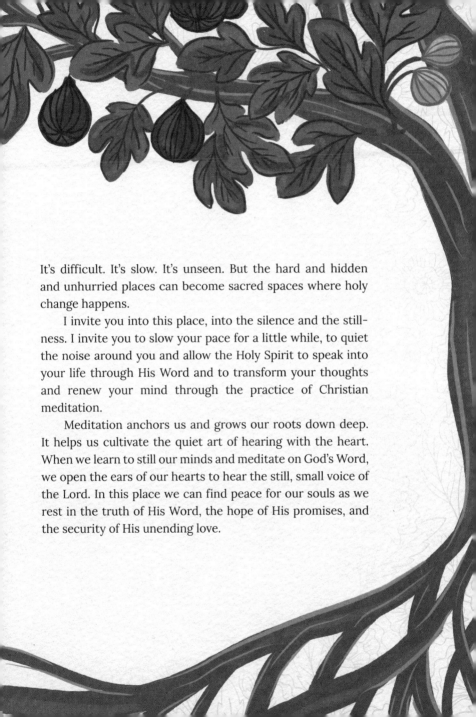

It's difficult. It's slow. It's unseen. But the hard and hidden and unhurried places can become sacred spaces where holy change happens.

I invite you into this place, into the silence and the stillness. I invite you to slow your pace for a little while, to quiet the noise around you and allow the Holy Spirit to speak into your life through His Word and to transform your thoughts and renew your mind through the practice of Christian meditation.

Meditation anchors us and grows our roots down deep. It helps us cultivate the quiet art of hearing with the heart. When we learn to still our minds and meditate on God's Word, we open the ears of our hearts to hear the still, small voice of the Lord. In this place we can find peace for our souls as we rest in the truth of His Word, the hope of His promises, and the security of His unending love.

CULTIVATE the QUIET ART of HEARING WITH THE HEART.

SILENCE AND STILLNESS
Slowing Down to Let God In

*In silence and in meditation on the eternal truths, I hear the
voice of God which excites our hearts to greater love.*
C. S. LEWIS

When was the last time you slowed down and sat in silence? Can you even remember the last time you set aside all the rushing and going and doing and instead let yourself sit still and just *be*?

How comfortable are you with stillness and silence?

If sitting still in complete silence isn't exactly your idea of fun, you're not alone. A study at the University of Virginia revealed that most people dislike being made to spend even six to fifteen minutes alone in a room with nothing to do but think. In fact, 67 percent of the men and 25 percent of the women *preferred to give themselves electric shocks rather than sit alone with their thoughts.*[1] Think we might have a problem?

Let's try a little experiment. To prepare, find a quiet and comfortable place to sit, and turn off any noise that may be around you. Then set a timer for five minutes.

Still your body.
Slow your breathing.
Inhale slowly and deeply.
Exhale slowly and fully.
Try to focus your mind on the present moment.
Simply sit in stillness and silence.

Stay that way until your timer goes off. Then come back here. . . .

Okay, so how did that go? Was it difficult? Easy? Relaxing? Stressful? What kinds of thoughts filled your mind?

Hopefully you didn't find yourself wanting to send a jolt of electricity through your body, but I bet you felt a bit uncomfortable for at least a moment or two. Maybe you checked the timer to see how much longer you had or you cut the time short so you could move along already. You probably found that your thoughts began to wander or your mind started racing. You may have become distracted, bored, or even sleepy.

If any of this reflects your experience of sitting in silence, welcome to the club!

Most of us have a hard time being still. We're always busy, moving, and doing. Even if our bodies aren't moving, our minds are always going, always working, always thinking. We don't often allow ourselves to sit alone in the quiet with our thoughts. Some of us even go out of our way to avoid it. Just the thought of being alone with our thoughts can be a rather unsettling proposition.

Besides, it's not hard to avoid silence. We live in a noisy and fast-paced world with packed schedules and little breathing room. Our days quickly fill with chores and errands, cooking and cleaning, work and school, kids and family. If we're lucky, we may even squeeze in a quick "quiet time" with God somewhere in the middle of it all. But there's no real space for silence. Even if we do have a bit of downtime, we typically fill it with noise and activities such as watching television, scrolling on our phones, or playing music.

We rarely truly embrace silence. And it shows.

Despite technology being more advanced than ever, our souls are suffering. We may seem more connected with cell phones in our pockets and social media at our fingertips, but the truth is we are actually less connected than ever.[2] Not only are we often lacking genuine, deep connections to others, but we lack a deep connection to our own selves and to the One who made us.

We want peace, but we want it fast. We want connection, but we settle for online distraction. We want to ease our stress and anxiety, but we want a quick fix so we can get on with our lives.

We've lost the art of being still, of living slow.

None of this is new or surprising. We know we're busy and distracted. We know we don't spend very much intentional time with God. We know we're not good at being still. But if we're honest, most of us don't see a realistic way to change. This is just the way it is. We may think to ourselves, *Someday things will slow down. Someday life won't be so crazy. Someday I'll have time to work on all that internal stuff. But right now there's just too much to do, too many other pressing and urgent needs.*

But waiting for "someday" leaves us with shallow roots.

We can't keep waiting for someday to come. Today is the day to start slowing down and making time to do the inner work that really matters—the soul-deep work of spiritual formation and soul care, the anchoring work of growing deep roots. Today is the day to take time to be still, to let God in, and to linger long in His presence.

MEDITATION AND MINDFULNESS
Being Present with Purpose

"Are you tired? Worn out? Burned out on religion? Come to me. Get away with me and you'll recover your life. I'll show you how to take a real rest. Walk with me and work with me—watch how I do it. Learn the unforced rhythms of grace. I won't lay anything heavy or ill-fitting on you. Keep company with me and you'll learn to live freely and lightly."
MATTHEW 11:28–30 MSG

Many practices can help us cultivate a habit of silence and stillness, but one that has been profoundly helpful to me personally is meditation. I have found that a regular practice of meditation can help nurture the spiritual habit of being still, gently guiding us to become comfortable with silence as we participate in the slow and holy process of spiritual growth.

There are many forms of meditation around the world, practiced for a variety of purposes. But as I've previously written,

Many of these practices often involve attempting to *empty* the mind or looking *within self* to find peace. These techniques may have some benefits, but mindfulness and meditation that is not centered in Christ and His love for us will not lead to true flourishing—it may help give our bodies a temporary reprieve from the physical symptoms of stress, but we miss out on the deeper connection our souls long to have with Christ.[3]

For this reason, I'm focusing in this book on two forms of meditation that have been most helpful to me, both in growing my faith and in strengthening my mental and spiritual health: *Christian meditation* and *mindfulness meditation*.

Christian meditation, particularly Scripture meditation, is a classical spiritual discipline rooted deeply in the Bible and in ancient Christian practice. Meditation is a way of communing with God through pondering His Word. J. I. Packer describes Christian meditation as "an activity of holy thought, consciously performed in the presence of God, under the eye of God, by the help of God, as a means of communion with God."[4]

Meditation is a holy habit that plays an important role in our spiritual growth. The Bible itself encourages us to meditate regularly: "This Book of the Law shall not depart from your mouth, but you shall meditate on it day and night, so that you may be careful to do according to all that is written in it" (Joshua 1:8 ESV). "Blessed is the one . . . whose delight is in the law of the LORD, and who meditates on his law day and night" (Psalm 1:1–2 NIV). "O God, we meditate on your unfailing love" (Psalm 48:9).

There are several key differences between Christian meditation and other Eastern religious forms of meditation:

Christian Meditation

IS	IS NOT
Rooted in the Word of God	Rooted in Eastern spirituality
Focused on filling the mind with God's Word	Focused on emptying the mind of all thought
About attachment to God	About detachment from self
A method of communing with God	A method of merging with "the universe"

Mindfulness meditation is an awareness practice that emphasizes paying attention to the present moment. It cultivates an openhearted awareness of our own thoughts and feelings, giving us a compassionate and effective way to intentionally change our patterns of thinking. Instead of ruminating on the past or rehearsing the future, we are able to rest in the present. This shift in focus changes the way we respond to stress and anxiety by training our brains to be less reactive and more reflective.

Mindfulness techniques are backed by research and are essentially nonspiritual, so as Christians we don't need to be wary of practicing mindfulness. In fact, mindfulness is a practice that can turn us toward God and help us experience greater peace. It's a way we can abide in Christ as we foster an intentional awareness of God's presence with us, right here and now.

Irene Kraegel describes it like this:

> Christian mindfulness is showing up where God is, in the present moment, and paying attention to all that is in that given moment so as not to miss God's renewal and healing. It is cultivating silent spaces for listening and awareness, releasing our tight grip on thoughts in order to open our hands to all that God provides in the moment.[5]

Mindfulness for the Christian isn't only about developing a present-moment awareness but about cultivating an every-moment awareness of God's presence with us.

Christian meditation and mindfulness can work together beautifully to help us draw near to God and experience His presence, while also helping us change unhelpful and negative thought patterns, and easing the physical and mental symptoms of anxiety and stress.

Christian Meditation + Mindfulness Meditation

CHRISTIAN MEDITATION	MINDFULNESS MEDITATION	TOGETHER
Contemplates God and His Word in everyday life	Develops present-moment awareness in everyday life	Help increase focus on God's presence with us in the moment
Helps direct our thoughts toward the things of God	Helps us notice our thoughts	Help us pay attention to our thoughts and change the way we think so we can develop more helpful and edifying thinking patterns
Cultivates Christlikeness	Cultivates compassion	Cultivate spiritual growth and produces the fruit of the Spirit in our lives
Supports spiritual health	Supports mental health	Benefits mind, body, and soul by reducing stress, calming anxiety, and helping us rest and experience greater peace

Meditation and mindfulness practices have been shown to rewire the neural pathways in our brains, creating new connections and changing the way we think and how we regulate our emotions. These changes overflow into our lives and have many proven benefits to our physical, mental, and spiritual well-being.

MENTAL AND PHYSICAL HEALTH BENEFITS[6]	SPIRITUAL BENEFITS
• Reduce stress • Improve sleep • Give a greater ability to cope with pain • Reduce symptoms of anxiety and depression • Decrease blood pressure • Lower resting heart rate • Promote emotional health and fewer negative thoughts • Rewire the brain and carve new neural pathways • Change the structure of the brain related to emotional regulation • Improve attention span and memory • Increase patience and distress tolerance • Increase imagination and creativity	• Deepen your faith • Help the Word of God take root in your heart and mind • Renew your mind as you turn and return to truth • Increase compassion toward yourself and others • Increase your knowledge of God • Deepen your awareness of the presence of God • Tune your heart to hear the still, small voice of the Holy Spirit • Increase spiritual formation toward Christlikeness • Cultivate the fruit of the Spirit in your life: love, joy, peace, patience, kindness, goodness, faithfulness, gentleness, and self-control (Galatians 5:22–23)

LECTIO DIVINA

A Framework for Christian Meditation

How can we pray to Him without being with Him? How can we be with Him unless we think of Him often? And how can we think of Him often unless we make this a holy habit?

BROTHER LAWRENCE

There are many different forms and methods of Christian meditation and a vast number of suggestions, plans, and guides for meditating on God's Word. The method I have personally found most helpful in cultivating my own spiritual rhythm of daily meditation is a centuries-old practice called *lectio divina*.

Lectio divina (Latin for "divine reading") is an ancient monastic practice introduced in the sixth century by Benedict of Nursia as a method of reading, praying, and meditating on Scripture that emphasized listening deeply "with the ear of your heart."[7] Although it is traditionally known as a monastic practice, many Christians today from a variety of traditions have found that it provides a helpful framework for meditation, a valuable practice for spiritual growth, and a way to "let the word of Christ dwell in you richly" (Colossians 3:16 ESV).

Lectio divina is a way to slow down and linger over Scripture, to savor the Word in a way that brings deep nourishment to the soul. In fact, many who practice it liken it to the process of eating: "Reading, as it were, puts the solid food into our mouths, meditation chews it and breaks it down, prayer obtains the flavour of it and contemplation is the very sweetness which makes us glad and refreshes us."[8] Lectio divina encourages a slow metabolizing of God's Word—rather than rushing through a quiet time, sampling little bits of Scripture or quickly consuming verses for the sake of checking off a list—so that it works into the very marrow of the soul, transforming the way we think and the way we live.

Traditionally, lectio divina is comprised of five parts: *silencio* (silence), *oratio* (pray), *lectio* (read), *meditatio* (meditate), and *contemplatio* (rest). Some modified versions, including the one I share in this book, include *incarnatio* (embody), which emphasizes the importance of transformation and assimilation of Scripture into the way we live.

The different elements of lectio divina are not necessarily steps that follow a sequential order, but more like interconnected movements. Think of it less like a staircase and more like a symphony. Each element plays a part, but they all work together in various combinations to create a rhythm of meditation and prayer. For example, there is not just one singular prayer; rather, multiple pauses for prayer are woven throughout the entire practice. The same is true for reading and meditating—there is a repeated, circling rhythm of reading, meditation, and prayer throughout.

Lectio divina isn't a mystical, subjective approach to God's Word. It's simply a framework, a rhythm, for prayerful meditation on Scripture. It is not by any means the only method. Even within the practice of lectio divina, there are several different modified versions that have been developed and used throughout the centuries and among various Christian traditions, from the Benedictine Christians all the way to modern-day Protestants and Orthodox Christians. And even though each variation has a slightly different cadence, the overall purpose is the same: to develop a spiritual rhythm of prayer and meditation that stills the soul, quiets the mind, and opens the heart to hear the voice of the Lord.

The lectio divina meditations in this book include the following five movements:

Lectio Divina
FRAMEWORK

Silencio
SILENCE

oratio
PRAY

lectio
READ

meditatio
MEDITATE

incarnatio
EMBODY

SILENCE (*SILENCIO*)

Quiet, everyone! Shh! Silence before GOD.
Something's afoot in his holy house. He's on the move!
ZECHARIAH 2:13 MSG

To meditate, we must first become a friend to silence. We have to quiet the noise so we can hear God's voice, focus our minds so we can notice our thoughts, and still our bodies so we can navigate our feelings.

And so we begin our meditation time by simply entering into a few minutes of stillness and silence. You will probably want to find a quiet, comfortable place to sit. Turn off any noises that may be around you. Still your body and slow your breath. Focus very simply on the present moment and on God's presence with you in this moment.

Simply be still in His presence. It's as simple, and as hard, as that.

Silence may very well just be the most difficult, and often the most uncomfortable, part of the meditation process. Silence opens the door to vulnerability. It's just you and God alone with your thoughts and emotions. If you don't have a lot of experience with that, it can be rather challenging and even sometimes distressing.

But this is where we begin because this is the soil of transformation. After all, it's in the dark and quiet places, away from the noise and the crowds, where real growth germinates and our roots reach down deep.

Henri Nouwen once wrote, "Solitude is the furnace of transformation."[9] In the fire of inner stillness and solitude, the outside noises fade as the chaff of your busy life burns away and the reality of what's really going on in your heart and mind can be revealed. This is what sets the stage for the Spirit to move in and water your soul, for you to open the ears of your heart and hear Him speak His word of life and love and grace into all the dark and hidden places.

Silence, particularly meditative silence, also provides us with an opportunity to change the way we think about our thoughts. When we are still, both without and within, we can observe our thoughts from a calm and compassionate posture, instead of being reactive or judgmental toward them. Over time, this practice gives us greater control over our thoughts, allowing us to more easily shift our thinking away from unhealthy or negative patterns and toward more edifying thoughts that will strengthen us both mentally and spiritually. In this way, the furnace becomes a friend as silence shifts from something uncomfortable and difficult to a time that brings genuine peace and rest to our minds and souls.

This kind of silence takes practice and patience. It's normal to feel uncomfortable. It's normal for your mind to wander. This doesn't mean you're failing. It's actually part of the process. And as with any new skill, it does get easier the more you practice.

If you struggle with stillness and silence, become overwhelmed by your thoughts, or are easily distracted, you may benefit from incorporating some simple mindfulness practices to learn how to handle those meandering thoughts and feelings and to redirect your focus back to the present moment. In the appendix, I share two of my favorite practices that I use regularly during times of meditation—breath prayer and trains of thought—to try during your own times of silent meditation.

PRAY (ORATIO)

"You will call to Me and come and pray to Me, and I will listen to you. You will seek Me and find Me when you search for Me with all your heart."
JEREMIAH 29:12–13 HCSB

Prayer is the element that binds all of lectio divina together. Prayer is woven in and through every movement of the practice because it is our primary method of communion with God as we meditate on His Word. Through prayer, we communicate with God. We speak to Him and we listen to Him. We ask questions and tell Him our thoughts. We respond to what we read in His Word, and we share whatever feelings arise. We wrestle, and we give thanks. We confess to Him, and we praise Him.

Prayer is not about stringing together the perfect sequence of words; it is simply honest communication with God. The goal of prayer is not to ferret out some kind of good feeling from God or get all the answers; it is to commune with the One who made you and loves you and invites you to give Him your burdens as you trust His heart and accept His grace.

Prayer is critical to the meditative process of lectio divina. In the meditations in this book, we will begin with an opening prayer, pause to pray throughout our reading and meditating, then close our time with a surrendering prayer. I've included guided prayers for the opening and surrendering prayers, but I encourage you to practice just talking to God from your own heart, in your own words. The prayers you pray as you meditate should be personal to you, depending on what the Holy Spirit reveals to you as you read and ponder His Word.

Try not to overthink your prayers. God already knows your heart. Even when our prayers are scattered and we're not sure what to say, the Holy Spirit helps us and intercedes for us (Romans 8:26–27). We simply need to open our hearts to God and share our questions and fears, our joys and desires, with Him.

READ (*LECTIO*)

My child, pay attention to what I say.
Listen carefully to my words.
Don't lose sight of them.
Let them penetrate deep into your heart,
for they bring life to those who find them,
and healing to their whole body.
PROVERBS 4:20–22

Reading God's Word is at the core of lectio divina. In fact, it is primarily what separates Christian meditation from other secular or Eastern meditative practices.

If silence is the soil that prepares our hearts to receive His Word, then the Scriptures are the vital nutrients that feed our souls. The heart of Christian meditation is to meditate on the Word of God, to fill our hearts with His Word, and to rest our souls in His presence.

In lectio divina, we read and reread a small passage of Scripture with a great deal of attention and focus. We are reading not to be informed, but to be transformed. This kind of reading isn't about accumulating facts but about assimilating God's Word into our very lives. As Eugene Peterson wrote, "We are not interested in knowing more but in becoming more."[10] We don't want to just *learn about* God; we want to *know* God. We want to draw close to Him and encounter Him through His Word in a way that changes us from the inside out.

Although lectio divina involves reading passages of Scripture, it is not the same as, nor is it a replacement for, Bible study. While Bible study typically engages our minds and intellect as we gain knowledge and understanding, lectio divina is more about engaging our hearts and souls as we commune with God through His Word. Studying God's Word is important and necessary to gain a comprehensive understanding of Scripture within the cultural and historical context of the passages and to discern theological meaning, but this kind of in-depth inductive study is not the purpose of lectio divina.

Ideally, passages used for lectio divina will flow out of a more in-depth time of studying Scripture so you aren't cherry-picking verses and losing proper interpretation of them. But for the purpose of this book, I've included a brief introduction with some context for each meditation passage.

You will read through a passage a total of three times (or more if you choose). Read slowly. Linger with the words. Abide with the Scripture.

When you read, you aren't trying to make anything happen or to force the passage to fit your preconceived preferences or opinions. The Bible is the living Word of God, a way for Him to speak to us personally through His Spirit as He transforms us and remakes us day by day to be more like Christ.

Simply read and linger on the words. Then, with each rereading of the passage, there is a meditative practice to consider, as well as a time to pause and pray. This is not a fast reading. It's a thoughtful and prayerful reading with the purpose of opening the ears of your heart to hear the voice of God.

MEDITATE (*MEDITATIO*)

Let the words of my mouth and the meditation of my heart be
acceptable in your sight, O Lord, my rock and my redeemer.
PSALM 19:14 ESV

Hand in hand with reading Scripture is the spiritual practice of meditating on it. Meditation on God's Word is what grows strong, deep roots of faith in our lives. It brings comfort as well as conviction, understanding as well as questions.

We should be careful to approach times of meditation with an attitude of submission to God and with an understanding that we are not trying to conjure a feeling or make something happen.

This process may be hard at times, when you don't feel as though any words stand out to you or you don't think the Holy Spirit is showing you anything at all. That's okay. Remember, meditation is not about perfection, and communion with God is not measured by how we feel. In these times when it doesn't "feel" as though meditation is working, continue to focus your heart and mind on reading the Scripture passage, sitting in the stillness, and praying as you contemplate what you read. You may not have a big takeaway. Try not to overthink it. The good news is that meditation doesn't end when you say the final prayer. You can continue to bring God's Word to mind throughout your day. You might be surprised at how the Holy Spirit will use His Word to meet you when you least expect it—and probably when you need it most.

No time spent meditating on Scripture is wasted time. This is a spiritual practice that will strengthen you from the inside out over time. It has a compounding effect—the more you consistently practice it, the greater the transformation you will notice in your life.

Meditation in the context of this book will be guided by three points of focus, each corresponding with its own reading of the Scripture passage and followed by prayer.

LECTIO 1

MEDITATION FOCUS: IDENTIFY ONE WORD OR PHRASE THAT STANDS OUT TO YOU. Read through the passage slowly, and consider just one word or phrase that stands out to you. Meditate on this word or phrase by holding it at the forefront of your thoughts. Pray as you consider the word, asking the Lord to help you hear what He is saying through His Word.

LECTIO 2

MEDITATION FOCUS: PRAY THE PASSAGE. Read through the passage a second time. This time you'll pray through the passage, reading phrase by phrase. Praying Scripture is another form of meditation, a way to slow down and linger over the words as you talk to God and respond to what you're reading while also allowing for times of silence. This will help you hear the Holy Spirit speaking to your heart as you meditate on His Word.

LECTIO 3

MEDITATION FOCUS: WHAT INVITATION IS GOD EXTENDING TO YOU TODAY? After reading the passage a third time, you will sit in stillness as you contemplate the word or phrase that stood out to you during the first reading and consider how it may apply to your life right now. Pay attention to your thoughts and feelings, and consider your current circumstances in light of what you read in God's Word. You may be surprised by the emotions that bubble to the surface or thoughts that come to your mind. Bring these thoughts and feelings to God in prayer. You can trust Him with whatever is going on in your life.

Contemplate what invitation God may be extending to you. Maybe He's inviting you to rest in Him or trust Him. Perhaps He's convicting your heart about something you need to confess. Or maybe He's simply inviting you to praise or give thanks.

This invitation is what will help guide you to the final phase of lectio divina: embodying what the Holy Spirit has revealed to you.

HOW DO YOU KNOW WHETHER YOU'RE HEARING FROM GOD?

It's important as we meditate on Scripture that we keep God's Word, not our own experiences or emotions, as our authority. Meditation is not about feeling good or reaching some emotional high. It's about listening to God as you read His Word and pray. But how can you know whether what stood out to you is from God? How do you know that the Holy Spirit is impressing something on your heart rather than your own thoughts or desires?

During the meditation process, simply read God's Word and sit in stillness as you listen and pray. Write down any thoughts that come to you, and consider what God might be saying to you. If you're unsure whether it was the Holy Spirit who impressed those thoughts, come back later with these points in mind:

- Ask whether what you heard lines up with the written Word of God. God will never tell you to do something that contradicts Scripture.
- Get counsel from someone who knows Scripture and theology well. Let them help you discern whether it aligns with God's Word.
- Pray for confirmation in the form of peace and clarity.

EMBODY (INCARNATIO)

The Holy Spirit produces this kind of fruit in our lives: love, joy, peace, patience, kindness, goodness, faithfulness, gentleness, and self-control.
GALATIANS 5:22-23

The ultimate goal of Scripture meditation is to live it out, or to embody it, in your life.

Jesus said, "I am the vine; you are the branches. If you remain in me and I in you, you will bear much fruit; apart from me you can do nothing" (John 15:5 niv). "A good tree produces good fruit, and a bad tree produces bad fruit. . . . Yes, just as you can identify a tree by its fruit, so you can identify people by their actions" (Matthew 7:17–20).

The natural consequence of being deeply rooted in Christ is bearing the fruit of His Spirit. We can identify those who abide in Christ—those who meditate on His Word and spend time communing with Him in prayer—by the way they live. They are known by the fruit of love, joy, peace, patience, kindness, goodness, faithfulness, gentleness, and self-control in their lives.

This is the real work of Christian meditation—not simply changing the way we think but transforming the way we live. When we embody what we read in the Word, we show the world what God is like. When our actions toward others—in our homes and communities, around the world, and even on the other side of the screen—reflect the love and mercy and grace and holiness of God, the world gets to see and experience the goodness of God through us.

Let His Word work its way into the marrow of who you are and "let God transform you into a new person by changing the way you think" (Romans 12:2). "Let the word of Christ dwell in you richly" (Colossians 3:16 esv). Let the Spirit who lives in you begin to live *through* you.

Bearing fruit is not something that requires an elaborate checklist or plan; it's not something we can achieve or produce on our own. It's the miraculous, transforming work of the Holy Spirit. Simply, the more we are with Christ, the more like Christ we will be.

THINK ABOUT THESE THINGS
Putting It into Practice

*And now, dear brothers and sisters, one final thing. Fix your thoughts on
what is true, and honorable, and right, and pure, and lovely, and admirable.
Think about things that are excellent and worthy of praise. Keep putting
into practice all you learned and received from me—everything you heard
from me and saw me doing. Then the God of peace will be with you.*

PHILIPPIANS 4:8–9

When we meditate, we turn our thoughts away from unhelpful
thinking patterns and shift away from ruminations of the past
and worries about the future. But we also need something to direct our
thoughts *toward.*

Philippians 4:8–9 gives us a helpful guide for the kinds of things
we should focus our thoughts on—the things we should meditate upon.
Think about these things. Put them into practice. And the God of peace
will be with you.

Sounds simple enough, right? But thoughts can be tricky. In an
effort to think about all the "right" kinds of things, it can be easy to
scrutinize and judge every single thought that comes into your mind
and heap shame on yourself because of any not-so-perfect thoughts.

Can I reach out and wrap my arms around you and offer you a bit of
grace here, a bit of freedom? The truth about thoughts is this: thoughts
are just thoughts. Even intrusive or unwanted thoughts hold no power

unless you give it to them. Ruminating, worrying, or stressing about negative or intrusive thoughts will only give them more power. To minimize their control over your mind, do what Paul described as "taking every thought captive" (2 Corinthians 10:5 HCSB). We do this not by obsessing over our thoughts but by simply being mindful of them—noticing their presence with an attitude of compassion and grace—then intentionally shifting them toward something healthier and more edifying. This takes a lot of practice. A mindfulness activity, such as trains of thought in the appendix, may be especially helpful.

As trains of thought pass through your mind, simply observe them. If it's an intrusive, negative, or dishonorable thought, let it ride right by. Don't climb aboard or try to explore it. Don't try to figure it out. As you let those thoughts pass by, intentionally turn your attention toward a different train, something more edifying for your mind and soul.

In the guided meditations in this book, we're going to hop onto some new "trains" and explore them a bit. Over time, this practice will help us be more intentional about the thought trains we choose to board and spend time on. Rather than focusing on the loud, anxious thoughts taking up so much of our attention and time, we can compassionately choose to turn our focus toward trains of thought that are more beneficial to us.

The thirty meditations in this book will focus on each of these categories from Philippians 4: what is true, honorable, right, pure, lovely, admirable, excellent, and worthy of praise. You'll see as we meditate through various passages that these themes of focus overlap in many ways, together creating a complete picture of the kind of thinking that will help our roots grow deep and help our minds find greater peace as we grow in our knowledge and trust of God.

As we move into these meditations, it's important to remember that meditation is a practice that takes practice. I recommend starting small. If you are just beginning, don't jump into a full thirty-minute meditation session every single day. You will likely become discouraged quickly and give up. It's okay to build the practice slowly. I've included thirty guided meditations in this book, enough for a full month, but you don't have to do a different one, or even a full one, every day. I suggest starting with just one meditation a week, focusing on one section every day. Meditate on a single Scripture passage, and then live with that text for the whole week, contemplating it periodically throughout your days. Narrow the passage to just a single verse or phrase. Memorize it. Pray it throughout your week. Then grow your meditative muscle by adding more time of focused meditation the next week.

SOME GENTLE REMINDERS BEFORE YOU BEGIN

YOU'RE NOT CHECKING OFF A LIST. YOU'RE CHANGING THE RHYTHM OF YOUR LIFE. Meditation is not merely a task on your daily to-do list. It's a practice in cultivating a new way of thinking and being. It's going to take time, patience, and consistent dedication.

YOU'RE NOT GATHERING INFORMATION. YOU'RE SEEKING TRANSFORMATION. The goal is not to fill your mind with facts but to transform your mind through the power of the Holy Spirit as you turn and return again and again to God and the truth in His Word. This is slow and holy work.

YOU'RE NOT REACHING FOR PERFECTION. YOU'RE RESTING IN HIS PRESENCE. Meditation is not about perfection but about presence. Simply commit to showing up and being present in the presence of God. Open the ears of your heart to hear His still, small voice, and know that He is with you. That is enough.

YOU'RE NOT ATTEMPTING TO CALM THE SEA. YOU'RE LEARNING TO NAVIGATE THE WAVES. Your mind is like a sea, and your thoughts and emotions are like waves. Sometimes they will be small and still, but sometimes they will be big and strong. You're not trying to still the entire sea or empty your mind of all thoughts and feelings; rather, you're learning to observe them with compassion and to navigate them by turning your eyes to Christ and letting Him guide you through.

YOU'RE NOT IN A HURRY. YOU'RE ON A JOURNEY. No need to rush or hurry. This is a process of growing and pruning and growing some more. You can't hurry the journey along any more than you can make a tree grow faster or a flower bloom on cue. Part of this process is learning to be comfortable in the discomfort of waiting and slow growth. Go slow and be consistent. Small steps every day will lead to great progress over time.

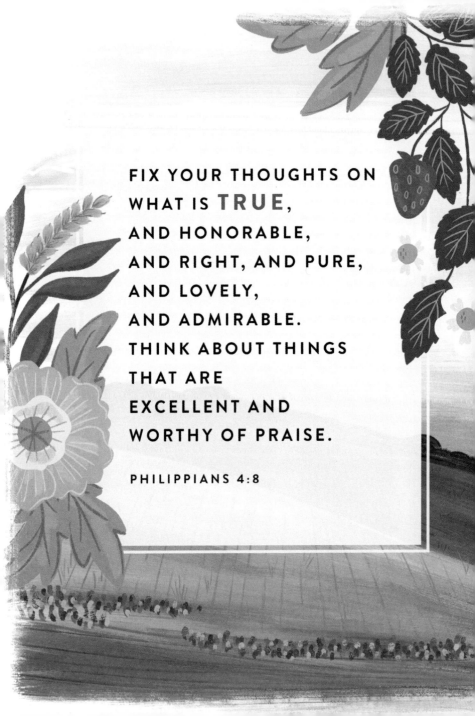

FIX YOUR THOUGHTS ON
WHAT IS **TRUE**,
AND HONORABLE,
AND RIGHT, AND PURE,
AND LOVELY,
AND ADMIRABLE.
THINK ABOUT THINGS
THAT ARE
EXCELLENT AND
WORTHY OF PRAISE.

PHILIPPIANS 4:8

WHATEVER
IS
true

WHATEVER IS TRUE

What is truth? It's the question Pontius Pilate asked Jesus right before sentencing Him to death (John 18:38), it's the question the serpent essentially presented to Eve in the garden while claiming that God had not really told them the truth (Genesis 3), and it's a question that is still asked in all kinds of ways today.

In a culture that encourages us to "live your truth" while our social media feeds and airwaves are flooded with vastly differing opinions and masses of misinformation, it's no wonder the actual truth can sometimes be difficult to discern.

Even our own feelings can betray us. Something may *feel* true, but that doesn't automatically mean it *is* true.

I may feel alone, but the truth is I am never really alone because God is always with me.

I may feel hopeless, but the truth is I can always have hope in God and the assurance of His promises.

I may feel worthless, but the truth is I have profound worth and value despite what I think or feel about myself.

I may even feel as though something I am doing is right because it makes me feel good or happy, but the truth is that sometimes choosing the thing that feels good in the moment might actually be harmful to myself or others in the long run.

Our feelings are real, but they don't always tell us the truth. We shouldn't ignore our feelings —after all, emotions are part of the incredible way God designed our bodies and minds, and they serve an important purpose—but we should be careful not to determine what is true solely on how we feel. Our feelings are not the foundation of truth.

The dictionary defines *truth* as "being in accord with fact or reality."[11] Truth is not based on feelings or opinions or assumptions. Truth is rooted in reality, in what actually is. As Christians, we believe the central reality that there is one true God who is the source of truth, and He has given us the gift of His Word to guide us and His Spirit to help us know what is true. In John 17:17, Jesus, speaking to the Father, said "Your word is truth" (NIV). To wisely discern what is true, you have to get the truth, God's Word, deep into the roots of your soul—meditate on it and "let God transform you into a new person by changing the way you think" (Romans 12:2).

This is not an easy task. It's hard work. Slow work. And the enemy will come at us with lies, with temptations to turn us away from truth. But if we learn to lean on God's Word and to really trust Him—with our thoughts and emotions and feelings and circumstances—we can learn to identify those lies and train our minds to instead turn toward what is true.

THE WORD OF GOD IS TRUE

PSALM 119:159–168

I f we're going to fix our minds on whatever is true, then God Himself and His Word should be our first focus. God's Word is the source of truth because God Himself is true.

David knew this. Over and over throughout the book of Psalms, we see him and other psalmists turn to God and His Word. Psalm 33:4 declares, "For the word of the Lord holds true, and we can trust everything he does," and Psalm 19:7 says, "The instructions of the Lord are perfect, reviving the soul." Psalm 119 in particular is filled with continual expressions of love for the instructions, laws, and promises of God. In fact, God's written revelation, His Word, is referred to in at least 171 of the 176 verses.

In verses 159–168 David expressed his love for God's Word—a love rooted in the firm belief that God can be trusted and everything He says is true. David also expressed his hatred for falsehood and lies, because lying is in opposition to truth and God's Word and doesn't produce anything good, but the love of truth—the love of God's instruction, of His Word—brings "abundant peace" (v. 165 HCSB).

Silence

Begin with a time of silence.

Still your body. . . . Slow your breathing. . . . Quiet your mind.

Focus on being fully present in this moment,
right here, right now.

the entirety of your word is truth.

Consider how I love your
precepts; LORD, give me life
according to your faithful love.
The entirety of your word is
truth, each of your righteous
judgments endures forever.
Princes have persecuted me
without cause, but my heart
fears only your word. I rejoice
over your promise like one who
finds vast treasure. I hate and
abhor falsehood, but I love
your instruction. I praise you
seven times a day for your
righteous judgments. Abundant
peace belongs to those who
love your instruction; nothing
makes them stumble. LORD,
I hope for your salvation and
carry out your commands.
I obey your decrees and love
them greatly. I obey your
precepts and decrees, for all
my ways are before you.

PSALM 119:159–168 CSB

Opening Prayer

God of all truth,

I bring my whole self to You right now—
    just as I am.
Help me to focus my mind on You today.
Turn my thoughts to the truth
    of Your Word.

I invite You to speak to me,
to search my heart and shape my life.
Show me what is true.

Open my eyes to see You.
Open my ears to hear Your voice.
Open my heart to receive Your Word.
Open my hands to accept whatever
    You give.

Draw close to me, Lord,
as I draw close to You.

Amen.

Read & Meditate

Read through the Bible passage three
times, taking time to pause and pray and
quietly listen to the Holy Spirit speaking
to your heart.

LECTIO 1: READ THROUGH THE PASSAGE SLOWLY.
What is one word or phrase that stands out to you?

> **PAUSE & PRAY**
> In silence, meditate on this word or phrase.

LECTIO 2: READ THROUGH THE PASSAGE A SECOND TIME.
This time, pray through the passage, reading phrase by phrase.
Talk to God, pausing to listen and respond to Him as you read.

> **PAUSE & PRAY**
> In silence, bring your attention to the present moment.

LECTIO 3: READ THROUGH THE PASSAGE A THIRD TIME.
Sit in stillness again as you contemplate the word or phrase that
stood out to you and how it may apply to your life right now.

> **NOTICE**
> Notice your body: What are you feeling right now?
> Notice your thoughts: What are you thinking right now?
> Notice your circumstances: What is happening in your life
> right now?

Compassionately consider these things, and listen to what the
Holy Spirit may be revealing to you in light of today's reading and
meditation. What invitation might God be extending to you today?

God is inviting me to . . .

Surrendering Prayer

As I prepare to enter into the rest of my day, Lord,

*Calm the lies in my head
and the fears that steal my peace.
Help me to turn my mind to truth
and to trust Your loving heart for me.*

*May my pace be slow and unhurried,
ever aware of Your presence with me.*

*May my mind be attentive and clear,
noticing the gift of every moment.*

*May my heart be gentle and kind,
showing compassion to myself and others.*

*Today, I give You my worries,
and I choose to trust the truth of Your Word.*

*Keep turning my thoughts to whatever is true.
Transform me to be more like You.*

Amen.

Embody

Continue to contemplate the word and invitation God gave you today.

Consider: What are some lies that your fears are telling you today? What truth can you intentionally focus on instead?

JESUS IS THE TRUTH

2

JOHN 14:1-6

At the last Passover meal, after Judas had left to commit his final act of betrayal, Jesus continued to speak to His disciples, telling them what was to come and giving them final instructions and words of comfort. He told them that He would not be with them much longer, that He had to go away. They were shocked and upset, filled with questions and struggling to understand what was about to happen.

Jesus saw their hearts and knew what they were thinking and feeling. He spoke to them with tender compassion, addressing their fears while assuring them that they would one day be with Him again. Jesus sees our hearts too. He knows our doubts and He sees our fears. And His answer to our troubled hearts is the same one He gave to the disciples when they wanted to know the way to where He was going: "I am the way, the truth, and the life."

We can follow Jesus because He is the way; we can trust Him because He is the truth; and we get to look forward to forever with Him because He is the life. When we focus our thoughts on Jesus as our ultimate truth, our hearts don't have to be troubled. We can lay worries and fears to rest in Him.

Silence

Begin with a time of silence.

Still your body. . . . Slow your breathing. . . . Quiet your mind.

Focus on being fully present in this moment,
right here, right now.

"Don't let your hearts be troubled. Trust in God, and trust also in me. There is more than enough room in my Father's home. If this were not so, would I have told you that I am going to prepare a place for you? When everything is ready, I will come and get you, so that you will always be with me where I am. And you know the way to where I am going."

"No, we don't know, Lord," Thomas said. "We have no idea where you are going, so how can we know the way?"

Jesus told him, "I am the way, the truth, and the life. No one can come to the Father except through me."

JOHN 14:1–6

Opening Prayer

Gracious Lord Jesus,

Though I'm surrounded by many troubles and hard things weigh heavy on my soul, I can breathe deeply knowing You are with me. I am not alone.

I invite You to speak to me, to search my heart and shape my life. Show me what is true.

Open my eyes to see You. Open my ears to hear Your voice. Open my heart to receive Your Word. Open my hands to accept whatever You give.

Draw close to me, Lord, as I draw close to You.

Amen.

Read & Meditate

Read through the Bible passage three times, taking time to pause and pray and quietly listen to the Holy Spirit speaking to your heart.

LECTIO 1: READ THROUGH THE PASSAGE SLOWLY.
What is one word or phrase that stands out to you?

PAUSE & PRAY
In silence, meditate on this word or phrase.

LECTIO 2: READ THROUGH THE PASSAGE A SECOND TIME.
This time, pray through the passage, reading phrase by phrase.
Talk to God, pausing to listen and respond to Him as you read.

PAUSE & PRAY
In silence, bring your attention to the present moment.

LECTIO 3: READ THROUGH THE PASSAGE A THIRD TIME.
Sit in stillness again as you contemplate the word or phrase that
stood out to you and how it may apply to your life right now.

NOTICE
Notice your body: What are you feeling right now?
Notice your thoughts: What are you thinking right now?
Notice your circumstances: What is happening in your life
right now?

Compassionately consider these things, and listen to what the
Holy Spirit may be revealing to you in light of today's reading and
meditation. What invitation might God be extending to you today?

God is inviting me to . . .

"I am the way,
the truth,
and the life."

JOHN 14:6

Surrendering Prayer

As I prepare to enter into the rest of my day, Lord,

I acknowledge that this day may be hard,
or this day may be easy.
No matter the way things go,
help me to keep trusting Your ways as I follow You.

May my pace be slow and unhurried,
ever aware of Your presence with me.

May my mind be attentive and clear,
noticing the gift of every moment.

May my heart be gentle and kind,
showing compassion to myself and others.

Today, I give You all that troubles my heart,
and I trust You with my life.

Keep turning my thoughts to whatever is true.
Transform me to be more like You.

Amen.

Embody

Continue to contemplate the word and invitation God gave you today.

Consider: What is troubling your heart today? What is a tangible way you can trust Jesus with those troubles?

....

....

....

3

REMAIN IN THE TRUTH

JOHN 15:1–5

Throughout the Old Testament, grapevines and vine-yards were often used as a visual representation of God's people, who were planted and tended by Him. When Jesus spoke to His disciples in John 15, He used this familiar imagery but with a critical reframe: He told them that *He* was the true vine, they were the branches, and a relationship with God was possible only through an attachment to *Him*.

In this passage, Jesus was about to go to the cross, and His disciples were about to face deep pain, fear, and confusion as they watched the One they had followed and loved be tortured and killed. This was not what they thought would happen when the Messiah arrived. This was not the way they wanted the story to go.

The disciples didn't know all that was coming. There was so much they didn't understand. But Jesus knew. And He knew what they would need most to remain strong and secure and rooted in truth, and He said to them, "Remain in me" (v. 4).

Silence

Begin with a time of silence.

Still your body. . . . Slow your breathing. . . . Quiet your mind.

Focus on being fully present in this moment,
right here, right now.

"the one who
remains in me
and I in him
produces much fruit."

JOHN 15:5 CSB

"I am the true vine, and my Father is the gardener. Every branch in me that does not produce fruit he removes, and he prunes every branch that produces fruit so that it will produce more fruit. You are already clean because of the word I have spoken to you. Remain in me, and I in you. Just as a branch is unable to produce fruit by itself unless it remains on the vine, neither can you unless you remain in me. I am the vine; you are the branches. The one who remains in me and I in him produces much fruit, because you can do nothing without me."

JOHN 15:1–5 CSB

Opening Prayer

Lord God, Gardener of my soul,

Tend my soul today as I turn my thoughts
    to You.
Clear my mind of the weeds that entangle
me, and help me to be fully present
    with You,
just as You are fully present with me.

I invite You to speak to me,
to search my heart and shape my life.
Show me what is true.

Open my eyes to see You.
Open my ears to hear Your voice.
Open my heart to receive Your Word.
Open my hands to accept whatever
    You give.

Draw close to me, Lord,
as I draw close to You.

Amen.

Read & Meditate

Read through the Bible passage three times, taking time to pause and pray and quietly listen to the Holy Spirit speaking to your heart.

LECTIO 1: READ THROUGH THE PASSAGE SLOWLY.
What is one word or phrase that stands out to you?

PAUSE & PRAY
In silence, meditate on this word or phrase.

LECTIO 2: READ THROUGH THE PASSAGE A SECOND TIME.
This time, pray through the passage, reading phrase by phrase.
Talk to God, pausing to listen and respond to Him as you read.

PAUSE & PRAY
In silence, bring your attention to the present moment.

LECTIO 3: READ THROUGH THE PASSAGE A THIRD TIME.
Sit in stillness again as you contemplate the word or phrase that
stood out to you and how it may apply to your life right now.

NOTICE
Notice your body: What are you feeling right now?
Notice your thoughts: What are you thinking right now?
Notice your circumstances: What is happening in your life
right now?

Compassionately consider these things, and listen to what the
Holy Spirit may be revealing to you in light of today's reading and
meditation. What invitation might God be extending to you today?

God is inviting me to . . .

Surrendering Prayer

As I prepare to enter into the rest of my day, Lord,

*May I remain in You and grow
with branches stretched toward You,
with fruit that bears Your character,
with roots that are strong and deep
and secure in Your truth and love.*

*May my pace be slow and unhurried,
ever aware of Your presence with me.*

*May my mind be attentive and clear,
noticing the gift of every moment.*

*May my heart be gentle and kind,
showing compassion to myself and others.*

*Today, I will release my need for control,
and I will simply abide in You.*

*Keep turning my thoughts to whatever is true.
Transform me to be more like You.*

Amen.

Embody

Continue to contemplate the word and invitation God gave you today.

Consider: What kind of fruit does your life bear right now? What's a practical way you can remain in Christ today?

....

....

....

TRUE LIVING IS EMPOWERED BY THE SPIRIT

4

JOHN 14:16–18, 26–27

In His final days on earth, when Jesus had to tell His disciples good-bye, He made it clear that even though He was leaving, He was not abandoning them. He would not be leaving them alone to fight the lies of Satan and the evils of the world. The Holy Spirit—"the Spirit of truth" (v. 17)—would be sent to dwell with them, bringing His power and counsel and help for all that they would face.

This promise is true for *all* believers. We get the gift of the Holy Spirit within us. Just as the Father abides in Jesus, the Spirit abides in us. Just as the Father is in close communion with the Son, so Jesus through the Spirit is in continual communion with us.

When life gets hard and the path is unclear, when difficult circumstances make the truth hard to see, we aren't left alone to figure it all out on our own. We have a Helper, the Holy Spirit, within us to lead us and guide us in the truth; we have the Comforter gently calming our troubled hearts and replacing our fear with His peace.

Silence

Begin with a time of silence.

Still your body. . . . Slow your breathing. . . . Quiet your mind.

Focus on being fully present in this moment,
right here, right now.

"I will ask the Father, and he will give you another advocate to help you and be with you forever—the Spirit of truth. The world cannot accept him, because it neither sees him nor knows him. But you know him, for he lives with you and will be in you. I will not leave you as orphans; I will come to you. . . .

"The Advocate, the Holy Spirit, whom the Father will send in my name, will teach you all things and will remind you of everything I have said to you. Peace I leave with you; my peace I give you. I do not give to you as the world gives. Do not let your hearts be troubled and do not be afraid."

JOHN 14:16–18, 26–27 NIV

Opening Prayer

My great and loving God,

You know my mind and my heart;
You see the truth of who I am.
Calm my anxious thoughts today.
Clear my mind so I can focus
on what is true.

I invite You to speak to me,
to search my heart and shape my life.
Show me what is true.

Open my eyes to see You.
Open my ears to hear Your voice.
Open my heart to receive Your Word.
Open my hands to accept whatever
*   You give.*

Draw close to me, Lord,
as I draw close to You.

Amen.

Read & Meditate

Read through the Bible passage three times, taking time to pause and pray and quietly listen to the Holy Spirit speaking to your heart.

LECTIO 1: READ THROUGH THE PASSAGE SLOWLY.
What is one word or phrase that stands out to you?

> **PAUSE & PRAY**
> In silence, meditate on this word or phrase.

LECTIO 2: READ THROUGH THE PASSAGE A SECOND TIME.
This time, pray through the passage, reading phrase by phrase.
Talk to God, pausing to listen and respond to Him as you read.

> **PAUSE & PRAY**
> In silence, bring your attention to the present moment.

LECTIO 3: READ THROUGH THE PASSAGE A THIRD TIME.
Sit in stillness again as you contemplate the word or phrase that
stood out to you and how it may apply to your life right now.

> **NOTICE**
> Notice your body: What are you feeling right now?
> Notice your thoughts: What are you thinking right now?
> Notice your circumstances: What is happening in your life
> right now?

Compassionately consider these things, and listen to what the
Holy Spirit may be revealing to you in light of today's reading and
meditation. What invitation might God be extending to you today?

God is inviting me to . . .

Surrendering Prayer

As I prepare to enter into the rest of my day, Lord,

I am so grateful for the gift of the Holy Spirit,
my Comforter, Advocate, Helper, and Guide.
Help me to be sensitive to Your guidance.
Empower me by Your Spirit to live what is true.

May my pace be slow and unhurried,
ever aware of Your presence with me.

May my mind be attentive and clear,
noticing the gift of every moment.

May my heart be gentle and kind,
showing compassion to myself and others.

Today, I give You my fears,
and I rest in the peace of Your presence.

Keep turning my thoughts to whatever is true.
Transform me to be more like You.

Amen.

Embody

Continue to contemplate the word and invitation God gave you today.

Consider: How are you listening to the Spirit of truth in your everyday life? When your day is particularly stressful, how can you intentionally pause and pay attention to the Spirit's guidance?

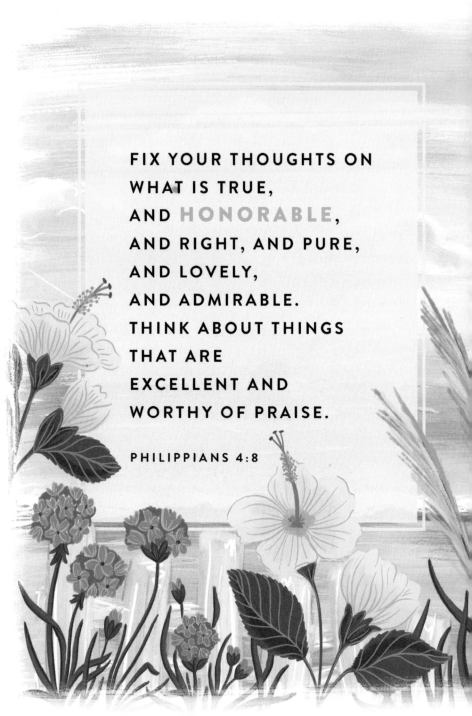

FIX YOUR THOUGHTS ON
WHAT IS TRUE,
AND HONORABLE,
AND RIGHT, AND PURE,
AND LOVELY,
AND ADMIRABLE.
THINK ABOUT THINGS
THAT ARE
EXCELLENT AND
WORTHY OF PRAISE.

PHILIPPIANS 4:8

WHATEVER
IS
honorable

WHATEVER IS HONORABLE

What is honorable? According to the dictionary, the word honorable means "deserving of respect or high regard; entitled to honor; of great renown."[12] Some Bibles translate this word as "noble" and others as "honest." Regardless, this word brings a sense of reverence and respect. It brings to mind something or someone worthy of being lifted up high and put in a place of honor.

To think about honorable things means to lift our thoughts above the dirt and grime of the world—the dishonesty, cruelty, sinfulness, immorality, and evil things—and instead focus our minds on things that bring honor to God. In Colossians 3:1-2, Paul says: "Since you have been raised to new life with Christ . . . think about the things of heaven, not the things of earth."

When we think about the "things of heaven," or what is honorable, our first focus is on God Himself, who is most worthy of honor. There is none like Him. He created all things, and He holds all things together. He is powerful and mighty, good and kind, wonderful beyond words. Even when things fall apart in our lives and we don't understand what God is doing—He is still worthy of our honor.

After meditating on the worthiness of God, we can consider how we honor Him in our lives and in how we treat others. Often, these thoughts come through our prayers and worship; we honor God when we thank Him and praise Him. We can turn thoughts into action in how we live. We honor God when we trust Him, when we obey Him, and when we turn to Him. And we also honor Him in how we see and think about others. We honor Him when we see the value—the *imago Dei*—in one another, when we lift each other up with respect and compassion and love.

Despite all the dishonorable and crummy things in this world, honorable things are still all around us. Look in your life for the things that are respectable and ethical, just and honest, upstanding and good. Look for whatever is honorable in the news, in your community, on your social media feed, in your family, and focus on these things, knowing they are but an echo of the One who is most worthy of honor.

And when you find yourself ruminating on things that are not so honorable—things that you wouldn't want lifted high and put on display—notice those thoughts, too, and gently turn away from them. Turn your mind back to things that are noble and good, honest and upright. Turn and keep turning back toward God and all His honorable ways.

5

GOD IS WORTHY OF HONOR

ISAIAH 40:25-28

In Isaiah 40, we find the people of God in exile. They had abandoned Yahweh and instead gave glory—the glory and honor that was God's alone—to idols. Their time of exile was not only a time of judgment for their sins but also a time of reflection and restitution.

In this passage, we now see Isaiah declaring to the people a time of restoration: God was going to restore them! Salvation was coming! A time would come when "the glory of the Lord will be revealed, and all people will see it together" (v. 5). Isaiah went on to praise the everlasting Lord and describe the Savior who would come to rescue them. He would be both a divine warrior who would deliver His people and a Shepherd who would lead and protect them.

During their exile, when the Israelites questioned whether God really saw their troubles, whether He really cared, Isaiah reminded them of God's nature, of who He was and who He is—worthy of honor for all He has done and all that He will do. After all, the fulfillment of God's promises was contingent not on the circumstances or strength of the people but on the character and power of God Himself.

Silence

Begin with a time of silence.

Still your body. . . . Slow your breathing. . . . Quiet your mind.

Focus on being fully present in this moment,
right here, right now.

THE Lord IS THE
EVERLASTING GOD,
THE CREATOR OF
ALL THE EARTH.
HE NEVER GROWS
WEAK OR WEARY.
NO ONE CAN
MEASURE THE
DEPTHS OF HIS
UNDERSTANDING.

ISAIAH 40:28

"To whom will you compare me? Who is my equal?" asks the Holy One.

Look up into the heavens. Who created all the stars? He brings them out like an army, one after another, calling each by its name. Because of his great power and incomparable strength, not a single one is missing. O Jacob, how can you say the LORD does not see your troubles? O Israel, how can you say God ignores your rights? Have you never heard? Have you never understood? The LORD is the everlasting God, the Creator of all the earth. He never grows weak or weary. No one can measure the depths of his understanding.

ISAIAH 40:25–28

Opening Prayer

Almighty God,

You are wonderful beyond words.
Your power and glory are beyond
*   compare.*
Help me to be fully present right now,
fully focused on You and Your
incomparable glory.

I invite You to speak to me,
to search my heart and shape my life.
Show me what is honorable.

Open my eyes to see You.
Open my ears to hear Your voice.
Open my heart to receive Your Word.
Open my hands to accept whatever
*   You give.*

Draw close to me, Lord,
as I draw close to You.

Amen.

Read & Meditate

Read through the Bible passage three times, taking time to pause and pray and quietly listen to the Holy Spirit speaking to your heart.

LECTIO 1: READ THROUGH THE PASSAGE SLOWLY.
What is one word or phrase that stands out to you?

> **PAUSE & PRAY**
> In silence, meditate on this word or phrase.

LECTIO 2: READ THROUGH THE PASSAGE A SECOND TIME.
This time, pray through the passage, reading phrase by phrase.
Talk to God, pausing to listen and respond to Him as you read.

> **PAUSE & PRAY**
> In silence, bring your attention to the present moment.

LECTIO 3: READ THROUGH THE PASSAGE A THIRD TIME.
Sit in stillness again as you contemplate the word or phrase that
stood out to you and how it may apply to your life right now.

> **NOTICE**
> Notice your body: What are you feeling right now?
> Notice your thoughts: What are you thinking right now?
> Notice your circumstances: What is happening in your life
> right now?

Compassionately consider these things, and listen to what the
Holy Spirit may be revealing to you in light of today's reading and
meditation. What invitation might God be extending to you today?

God is inviting me to . . .

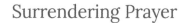

Surrendering Prayer

As I prepare to enter into the rest of my day, Lord,

May my pace be slow and unhurried,
ever aware of Your presence with me.

May my mind be attentive and clear,
noticing the gift of every moment.

May my heart be gentle and kind,
showing compassion to myself and others.

My understanding is like a tiny seed
in Your vast garden of wisdom.
There is so much I don't know, so much I don't understand.
But Your strength is infinite, and Your understanding is limitless.
You hear all my questions, and You know all my fears.

Today, I praise You and I honor You;
increase my faith as I learn to trust You more.

Keep turning my thoughts to whatever is honorable.
Transform me to be more like You.

Amen.

Embody

Continue to contemplate the word and invitation God gave you today.

Consider: What circumstances in your life make you feel as though God doesn't really see your troubles or care about your pain? How can you honor Him and trust Him more?

JESUS IS WORTHY OF HONOR

6

HEBREWS 1:3-4, 10-12

The author of Hebrews wrote this letter to a group of early Christians to address false teachings emerging among these believers and to strengthen their wavering faith. This community of believers was likely suffering persecution because of their new faith. Things were hard for these new believers, and they were struggling and suffering. But before addressing the specific issues they were facing, the author has them turn their attention to Jesus.

In times of suffering, we can look to Jesus. We can turn our thoughts to the One who is most worthy of honor.

The beginning of this letter boldly clarifies exactly who Jesus is, setting Him apart from previous prophets and religious leaders and establishing Him as greater than the angels. Jesus is the divine and incarnate Son of God. He sits at the place of honor at the right hand of God. He should be the focus of our highest honor and worship. If we want to fix our thoughts on whatever is honorable, let's fix our eyes and our hearts on Jesus.

Silence

Begin with a time of silence.

Still your body. . . . Slow your breathing. . . . Quiet your mind.

Focus on being fully present in this moment,
right here, right now.

The Son radiates God's own glory and expresses the very character of God, and he sustains everything by the mighty power of his command. When he had cleansed us from our sins, he sat down in the place of honor at the right hand of the majestic God in heaven. This shows that the Son is far greater than the angels. . . .

[God] also says to the Son, "In the beginning, Lord, you laid the foundation of the earth and made the heavens with your hands. They will perish, but you remain forever. They will wear out like old clothing. You will fold them up like a cloak and discard them like old clothing. But you are always the same; you will live forever."

HEBREWS 1:3–4, 10–12

Opening Prayer

Jesus, Light of the World,

There is no one like You.
You radiate the glory of God.
Shine Your light into my life today.
Light up all the dark places with Your
glorious presence.

I invite You to speak to me,
to search my heart and shape my life.
Show me what is honorable.

Open my eyes to see You.
Open my ears to hear Your voice.
Open my heart to receive Your Word.
Open my hands to accept whatever
*   You give.*

Draw close to me, Lord,
as I draw close to You.

Amen.

Read & Meditate

Read through the Bible passage three times, taking time to pause and pray and quietly listen to the Holy Spirit speaking to your heart.

LECTIO 1: READ THROUGH THE PASSAGE SLOWLY.
What is one word or phrase that stands out to you?

PAUSE & PRAY
In silence, meditate on this word or phrase.

LECTIO 2: READ THROUGH THE PASSAGE A SECOND TIME.
This time, pray through the passage, reading phrase by phrase.
Talk to God, pausing to listen and respond to Him as you read.

PAUSE & PRAY
In silence, bring your attention to the present moment.

LECTIO 3: READ THROUGH THE PASSAGE A THIRD TIME.
Sit in stillness again as you contemplate the word or phrase that
stood out to you and how it may apply to your life right now.

NOTICE
Notice your body: What are you feeling right now?
Notice your thoughts: What are you thinking right now?
Notice your circumstances: What is happening in your life
right now?

Compassionately consider these things, and listen to what the
Holy Spirit may be revealing to you in light of today's reading and
meditation. What invitation might God be extending to you today?

God is inviting me to . . .

The Son Radiates God's own glory and expresses the very character of God, and he sustains everything by the mighty power of his command.

HEBREWS 1:3

Surrendering Prayer

As I prepare to enter into the rest of my day, Lord,

May my pace be slow and unhurried,
ever aware of Your presence with me.

May my mind be attentive and clear,
noticing the gift of every moment.

May my heart be gentle and kind,
showing compassion to myself and others.

Jesus, You are the Maker and Sustainer of all things.
You are the anchor of my soul,
a sure and steady Rock through every storm.

Today, I release the need to try so hard to keep it all together,
and I rest in You, the keeper of my soul,
knowing You hold me safe and secure.

Keep turning my thoughts to whatever is honorable.
Transform me to be more like You.

Amen.

Embody

Continue to contemplate the word and invitation God gave you today.

Consider: How can you invite Jesus, the divine and incarnate Son of God, into the messy parts of your life? How can you show that He is worthy of honor today?

7

WE HONOR GOD BY HOW WE LIVE

1 PETER 2:7–12

The apostle Peter wrote to several churches who were facing persecution for their faith. He reminded them that even though they were facing all kinds of trials and were tempted to despair, there was more happening than they could see. He told them that in their suffering and rejection, they were sharing the fate of Jesus. Peter described Jesus as "the stone that the builders rejected," who had become the cornerstone of God's spiritual temple (v. 7). He went on to say, "They stumble because they do not obey God's word, and so they meet the fate that was planned for them" (v. 8).

We can respond to Jesus in one of two ways: either we make Him our cornerstone that serves as the reference by which we line up our lives, or He will be a stone that we stumble and trip over instead.[13]

With Christ as our cornerstone, we can honor Him with the way we live. We don't have to stumble around in the ways of the world anymore. The more we turn our thoughts to God's Word and the honorable things of God, the more they will influence how we live, steering us away from despair and closer to the heart of God.

Silence

Begin with a time of silence.

Still your body. . . . Slow your breathing. . . . Quiet your mind.

Focus on being fully present in this
moment, right here, right now.

You can show others
the goodness of God.

1 PETER 2:9

You are a chosen people. You are royal priests, a holy nation, God's very own possession. As a result, you can show others the goodness of God, for he called you out of the darkness into his wonderful light.

"Once you had no identity as a people; now you are God's people. Once you received no mercy; now you have received God's mercy."

Dear friends, I warn you as "temporary residents and foreigners" to keep away from worldly desires that wage war against your very souls. Be careful to live properly among your unbelieving neighbors. Then even if they accuse you of doing wrong, they will see your honorable behavior, and they will give honor to God when he judges the world.

1 PETER 2:9–12

Opening Prayer

Loving and merciful God,

Still my soul in Your presence today.
Show me Your goodness and grace.
Help me set aside my worries and fears
and rest in Your wonderful presence.

I invite You to speak to me,
to search my heart and shape my life.
Show me what is honorable.

Open my eyes to see You.
Open my ears to hear Your voice.
Open my heart to receive Your Word.
Open my hands to accept whatever
      You give.

Draw close to me, Lord,
as I draw close to You.

Amen.

Read & Meditate

Read through the Bible passage three times, taking time to pause and pray and quietly listen to the Holy Spirit speaking to your heart.

LECTIO 1: READ THROUGH THE PASSAGE SLOWLY.
What is one word or phrase that stands out to you?

....

> **PAUSE & PRAY**
> In silence, meditate on this word or phrase.

LECTIO 2: READ THROUGH THE PASSAGE A SECOND TIME.
This time, pray through the passage, reading phrase by phrase.
Talk to God, pausing to listen and respond to Him as you read.

> **PAUSE & PRAY**
> In silence, bring your attention to the present moment.

LECTIO 3: READ THROUGH THE PASSAGE A THIRD TIME.
Sit in stillness again as you contemplate the word or phrase that
stood out to you and how it may apply to your life right now.

> **NOTICE**
> Notice your body: What are you feeling right now?
> Notice your thoughts: What are you thinking right now?
> Notice your circumstances: What is happening in your life
> right now?

Compassionately consider these things, and listen to what the
Holy Spirit may be revealing to you in light of today's reading and
meditation. What invitation might God be extending to you today?

God is inviting me to . . .

....

....

....

Surrendering Prayer

As I prepare to enter into the rest of my day, Lord,

May my pace be slow and unhurried,
ever aware of Your presence with me.

May my mind be attentive and clear,
noticing the gift of every moment.

May my heart be gentle and kind,
showing compassion to myself and others.

You have rescued me from darkness
and brought me into Your wonderful light.
May my life reflect Your goodness,
and may my words be filled with Your grace.

Today, I set aside my pride and selfishness,
and I seek to honor You in all that I do.

Keep turning my thoughts to whatever is honorable.
Transform me to be more like You.

Amen.

Embody

Continue to contemplate the word and invitation God gave you today.

Consider: What is the evidence of God's light in your life? What is a tangible thing you can do to honor God and shine His light into the lives of those you encounter at work, at school, in the car, at home?

HONORABLE LIVING
HONORS OTHERS

8

ROMANS 9-10, 13-17

In Romans 12, Paul wrote about the church as the body of Christ. As in a human body, many parts (or members) make up one unified whole. We are connected to other believers in a larger sense, and God wants us to use the various gifts He gave us to love and serve one another.

Paul encouraged believers to not only show honor to God but also to "take delight in honoring each other" (v. 10, *emphasis mine*). If we focus our thoughts on how we can better love and honor one another, it leaves little room for cursing or disparaging each other. The English Standard Version of this verse tells us to "outdo one another in showing honor." What a beautiful picture it would be if we were known for one-upping each other in how we show honor!

Silence

Begin with a time of silence.

Still your body. . . . Slow your breathing. . . . Quiet your mind.

Focus on being fully present in this moment,
right here, right now.

*Don't just pretend to love
others. Really love them.
Hate what is wrong. Hold
tightly to what is good. Love
each other with genuine
affection, and take delight in
honoring each other. . . .
When God's people are in
need, be ready to help them.
Always be eager
to practice hospitality.
Bless those who persecute
you. Don't curse them; pray
that God will bless them. Be
happy with those who are
happy, and weep with those
who weep. Live in harmony
with each other. Don't be too
proud to enjoy the company
of ordinary people. And don't
think you know it all!
Never pay back evil with
more evil. Do things in such
a way that everyone can see
you are honorable.*

ROMANS 12:9–10, 13–17

Opening Prayer

Compassionate Lord,

*I bring my whole self to You today—
    just as I am.
Breathe Your breath of peace into my soul
as I quietly keep company with You.*

*I invite You to speak to me,
to search my heart and shape my life.
Show me what is honorable.*

*Open my eyes to see You.
Open my ears to hear Your voice.
Open my heart to receive Your Word.
Open my hands to accept whatever
    You give.*

*Draw close to me, Lord,
as I draw close to You.*

Amen.

Read & Meditate

Read through the Bible passage three
times, taking time to pause and pray and
quietly listen to the Holy Spirit speaking
to your heart.

LECTIO 1: READ THROUGH THE PASSAGE SLOWLY.
What is one word or phrase that stands out to you?

PAUSE & PRAY
In silence, meditate on this word or phrase.

LECTIO 2: READ THROUGH THE PASSAGE A SECOND TIME.
This time, pray through the passage, reading phrase by phrase.
Talk to God, pausing to listen and respond to Him as you read.

PAUSE & PRAY
In silence, bring your attention to the present moment.

LECTIO 3: READ THROUGH THE PASSAGE A THIRD TIME.
Sit in stillness again as you contemplate the word or phrase that
stood out to you and how it may apply to your life right now.

NOTICE
Notice your body: What are you feeling right now?
Notice your thoughts: What are you thinking right now?
Notice your circumstances: What is happening in your life
right now?

Compassionately consider these things, and listen to what the
Holy Spirit may be revealing to you in light of today's reading and
meditation. What invitation might God be extending to you today?

God is inviting me to . . .

TAKE
DELIGHT
in
HONORING
EACH OTHER.

ROMANS 12:10

Surrendering Prayer

As I prepare to enter into the rest of my day, Lord,

May my pace be slow and unhurried,
ever aware of Your presence with me.

May my mind be attentive and clear,
noticing the gift of every moment.

May my heart be gentle and kind,
showing compassion to myself and others.

Make my life more fruitful and my character more beautiful,
my soul more peaceful and my mind more tranquil,
as I seek to live an honorable life
by honoring You and honoring others.

Today, I lay down my pride, which separates me from others,
and I accept the gift of community
and look for ways to honor and serve those around me.

Keep turning my thoughts to whatever is honorable.
Transform me to be more like You.

Amen.

Embody

Continue to contemplate the word and invitation God gave you today.

Consider: How can you lavishly honor the people in your life, both those who are easier and those who are harder to love?

....

....

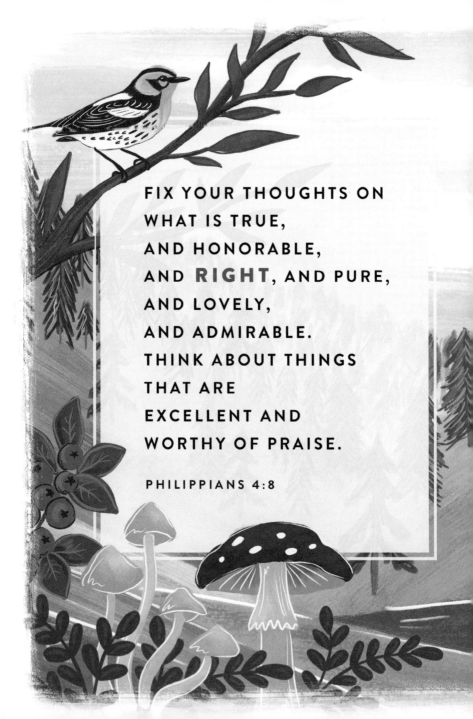

FIX YOUR THOUGHTS ON
WHAT IS TRUE,
AND HONORABLE,
AND **RIGHT**, AND PURE,
AND LOVELY,
AND ADMIRABLE.
THINK ABOUT THINGS
THAT ARE
EXCELLENT AND
WORTHY OF PRAISE.

PHILIPPIANS 4:8

WHATEVER
IS
right

WHATEVER IS RIGHT

What is right? The word *right* is defined as "being in accordance with what is just, good, or proper."[14] We often think of it in terms of right versus wrong or good versus bad. And if we're honest, it can be easy to let the "wrong" things overwhelm us and to quickly become filled with fear and anxiety when we see so much in our world that is not right or just. A quick scroll through the news any day of the week reveals depravity, tragedy, injustice, and inequality all around the world. Crime and violence, selfishness and greed, lust and pride, are seemingly everywhere we turn. And things in our own lives might not be "right" either—things that are unfair, painful, and broken, things that can easily tempt us to worry or despair.

So how do we keep our thoughts focused on what is right when we're surrounded by so much that is wrong?

It's important to note that turning our minds to whatever is right doesn't mean pretending that nothing is wrong. It doesn't mean denying reality or ignoring the injustice or evil of this world. It means that when things are wrong or when we're tempted to dwell on those things, we turn our attention to Christ, the holy and righteous One who is always just and good. It means that when darkness surrounds us, we keep our eyes on the Light and then live as a light *in the midst of* the darkness.

Mindful awareness of the presence of Christ—Light Himself—with us and within us, even when surrounded by darkness, can help shift us away from feelings of anxiety and worry over all that is wrong and toward an abiding inner peace as we trust in the One who is wholly righteous and just in all His ways.

Turning our thoughts to whatever is right is not always easy. Sometimes trains of thought pass through our minds that tempt us toward what is wrong. Thoughts may tempt us to cheat or lie, to turn away when we see injustice, or to lash out with hurtful words when we're angry. But just because a train pulls into the station doesn't mean you have to jump on it. Just because a thought enters your mind doesn't mean you have to indulge it and linger with it. Instead, simply let those thoughts pass right by, and turn toward the ones that will draw you closer to Christ.

Romans 3:10 reminds us, "No one is righteous—not even one." Not a single one of us does and thinks what is right 100 percent of the time. We can let go of that unrealistic expectation of perfection. It's about direction, not perfection. As you turn your thoughts, you'll find your life turning too. As you meditate on what is right, even in the midst of so much that is wrong, you'll find the courage and strength to reflect the righteousness of Christ to a world that needs it.

GOD DOES WHAT IS RIGHT

Our passage today is found in the middle of four chapters known as Isaiah's "apocalypse," in which the prophet Isaiah "introduces God's universal judgment, the renewal of the earth, the removal of death and the effects of sin, the deliverance of his people, and the victorious and universal rule of God."[15] We are reminded that in all that has been, in all that is now, and in all that is still to come, God will bring justice and deliver His creation and His people.

This particular passage is part of what some scholars identify as the "song of the redeemed," written to those who trusted Yahweh, and it was a message of thanksgiving and celebration of trust in God. While Isaiah was aware that it could be a long time before God's plans and purposes were fully realized on earth, he offered encouragement to endure through difficulty and remain faithful, reminding the people to keep their thoughts fixed on God. He reminded them, too, that God could be trusted, that He is just in His judgments, and that He will always do what is right.

Silence

Begin with a time of silence.

Still your body. . . . Slow your breathing. . . . Quiet your mind.

Focus on being fully present in this moment,
right here, right now.

You are
a God
who does
what is
Right.

ISAIAH 26:7

You will keep in perfect peace all who trust in you, all whose thoughts are fixed on you! Trust in the LORD always, for the LORD GOD is the eternal Rock. He humbles the proud and brings down the arrogant city. He brings it down to the dust. The poor and oppressed trample it underfoot, and the needy walk all over it. But for those who are righteous, the way is not steep and rough. You are a God who does what is right, and you smooth out the path ahead of them. LORD, we show our trust in you by obeying your laws; our heart's desire is to glorify your name.

ISAIAH 26:3-8

Opening Prayer

Righteous and holy God,

I set aside all the stressors that are pressing in
and all the worries that are
weighing me down.
Meet me here in this moment,
and fill my mind with the comfort of
Your Word.

I invite You to speak to me,
to search my heart and shape my life.
Show me what is right.

Open my eyes to see You.
Open my ears to hear Your voice.
Open my heart to receive Your Word.
Open my hands to accept whatever
You give.

Draw close to me, Lord,
as I draw close to You.

Amen.

Read & Meditate

Read through the Bible passage three times, taking time to pause and pray and quietly listen to the Holy Spirit speaking to your heart.

LECTIO 1: READ THROUGH THE PASSAGE SLOWLY.
What is one word or phrase that stands out to you?

PAUSE & PRAY
In silence, meditate on this word or phrase.

LECTIO 2: READ THROUGH THE PASSAGE A SECOND TIME.
This time, pray through the passage, reading phrase by phrase.
Talk to God, pausing to listen and respond to Him as you read.

PAUSE & PRAY
In silence, bring your attention to the present moment.

LECTIO 3: READ THROUGH THE PASSAGE A THIRD TIME.
Sit in stillness again as you contemplate the word or phrase that
stood out to you and how it may apply to your life right now.

NOTICE
Notice your body: What are you feeling right now?
Notice your thoughts: What are you thinking right now?
Notice your circumstances: What is happening in your life
right now?

Compassionately consider these things, and listen to what the
Holy Spirit may be revealing to you in light of today's reading and
meditation. What invitation might God be extending to you today?

God is inviting me to . . .

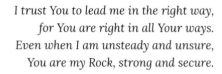

Surrendering Prayer

As I prepare to enter into the rest of my day, Lord,

I trust You to lead me in the right way,
for You are right in all Your ways.
Even when I am unsteady and unsure,
You are my Rock, strong and secure.

May my pace be slow and unhurried,
ever aware of Your presence with me.

May my mind be attentive and clear,
noticing the gift of every moment.

May my heart be gentle and kind,
showing compassion to myself and others.

Today, I lay down my plans,
and I embrace Your promises.

Keep turning my thoughts to whatever is right.
Transform me to be more like You.

Amen.

Embody

Continue to contemplate the word and invitation God gave you today.

Consider: What thing in your life doesn't seem to be going right at all? How can you trust God to do what is right, even in that circumstance?

FAITH MAKES US RIGHT IN GOD'S SIGHT

10

ROMANS 3:22-24, 27-28

I n this passage of Romans, Paul very clearly stated that we are made right with God by faith in Jesus Christ. This assertion was a massive shift for the Jews. Prior to Jesus, obeying the Mosaic law was paramount. But Jesus, the Messiah, changed everything.

Salvation is now a free gift, paid for with Jesus' blood and sealed with His resurrection. And this gift is offered not just to the Jews—it is for *everyone*. God's redemptive work on the cross and through the resurrection of Jesus took place apart from the law (v. 21) and is for both the gentiles who do not have the law and for the Jews who do not obey the law. This includes me and you!

Does that mean the law doesn't matter anymore? Not at all. The law reveals that we all fall short of God's perfect standard; it shows us our need for Jesus. Jesus is the fulfillment of the law, and now through Him we can fulfill the law. We get to do what is right, not in order to be made righteous but to reveal the righteousness we have already received through Christ.

Silence

Begin with a time of silence.

Still your body. . . . Slow your breathing. . . . Quiet your mind.

Focus on being fully present in this moment, right here, right now.

We are made right with God by placing our faith in Jesus Christ. And this is true for everyone who believes, no matter who we are. For everyone has sinned; we all fall short of God's glorious standard. Yet God, in his grace, freely makes us right in his sight. He did this through Christ Jesus when he freed us from the penalty for our sins....

Can we boast, then, that we have done anything to be accepted by God? No, because our acquittal is not based on obeying the law. It is based on faith. So we are made right with God through faith and not by obeying the law.

ROMANS 3:22–24, 27–28

Opening Prayer

Savior of my soul,

I come to You with holy boldness.
I know You hear my prayers.
You love me with an everlasting love.
You saved me by Your indescribable grace.

I invite You to speak to me,
to search my heart and shape my life.
Show me what is right.

Open my eyes to see You.
Open my ears to hear Your voice.
Open my heart to receive Your Word.
Open my hands to accept whatever
*   You give.*

Draw close to me, Lord,
as I draw close to You.

Amen.

Read & Meditate

Read through the Bible passage three times, taking time to pause and pray and quietly listen to the Holy Spirit speaking to your heart.

LECTIO 1: READ THROUGH THE PASSAGE SLOWLY.
What is one word or phrase that stands out to you?

PAUSE & PRAY
In silence, meditate on this word or phrase.

LECTIO 2: READ THROUGH THE PASSAGE A SECOND TIME.
This time, pray through the passage, reading phrase by phrase.
Talk to God, pausing to listen and respond to Him as you read.

PAUSE & PRAY
In silence, bring your attention to the present moment.

LECTIO 3: READ THROUGH THE PASSAGE A THIRD TIME.
Sit in stillness again as you contemplate the word or phrase that
stood out to you and how it may apply to your life right now.

NOTICE
Notice your body: What are you feeling right now?
Notice your thoughts: What are you thinking right now?
Notice your circumstances: What is happening in your life
right now?

Compassionately consider these things, and listen to what the
Holy Spirit may be revealing to you in light of today's reading and
meditation. What invitation might God be extending to you today?

God is inviting me to . . .

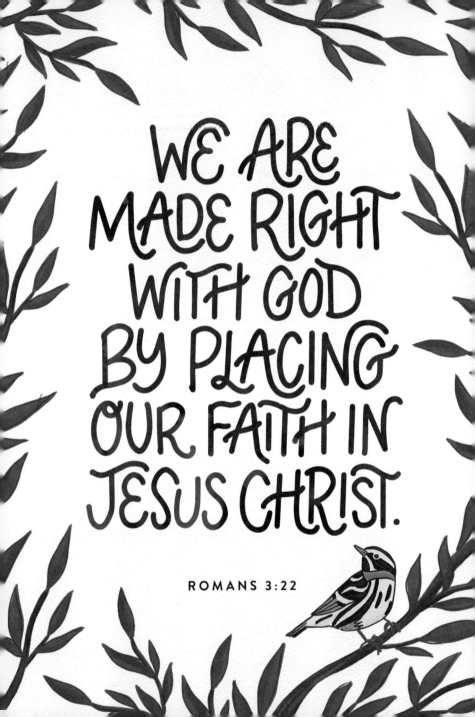

WE ARE MADE RIGHT WITH GOD BY PLACING OUR FAITH IN JESUS CHRIST.

ROMANS 3:22

Surrendering Prayer

As I prepare to enter into the rest of my day, Lord,

May the faith that saved me be the faith that shapes me.

The evidence of my salvation is not found in my feelings,
but it is rooted in Your promise and secured by Your love.

May my pace be slow and unhurried,
ever aware of Your presence with me.

May my mind be attentive and clear,
noticing the gift of every moment.

May my heart be gentle and kind,
showing compassion to myself and others.

Today, I want to stay near the cross.
You gave Your life for me, and I want to live my life for You.

Keep turning my thoughts to whatever is right.
Transform me to be more like You.

Amen.

Embody

Continue to contemplate the word and invitation God gave you today.

Consider: What evidence of faith is there in your life right now? In what ways might you still be trying to "earn" salvation?

....

....

11

PUT ON YOUR NEW RIGHTEOUS NATURE

EPHESIANS 4:21-24, 31-32

When we are made right with God through Jesus, we can live right, through the power of the Spirit we now have within us—the Holy Spirit, who transforms us from the inside out as we shed our old sinful nature and put on a "new nature, created to be like God—truly righteous and holy" (v. 24).

In this passage from Ephesians, Paul urged his readers to "walk in a manner worthy of the calling to which you have been called" (v. 1 ESV) and to "make every effort to keep the unity of the Spirit through the bond of peace" (v. 3 NIV). He spoke both of personal righteousness and individual growth as well as unity among members of the body of Christ.

Following Jesus will mean complete transformation, and it begins with letting the Spirit renew our thoughts and attitudes (v. 23). Changing our thought patterns and old ways of thinking will naturally change the way we live. Conversely, when we practice new ways of living by developing new habits and doing the right things even when we don't feel like it or when it isn't easy, our ways of thinking will begin to change as well.

Silence

Begin with a time of silence.

Still your body. . . . Slow your breathing. . . . Quiet your mind.

Focus on being fully present in this moment, right here, right now.

Put on your new nature, created to be like God — truly righteous and holy.

EPHESIANS 4:24

Since you have heard about Jesus and have learned the truth that comes from him, throw off your old sinful nature and your former way of life, which is corrupted by lust and deception. Instead, let the Spirit renew your thoughts and attitudes. Put on your new nature, created to be like God—truly righteous and holy. . . .

Get rid of all bitterness, rage, anger, harsh words, and slander, as well as all types of evil behavior. Instead, be kind to each other, tenderhearted, forgiving one another, just as God through Christ has forgiven you.

EPHESIANS 4:21–24, 31–32

Opening Prayer

Faithful and loving Father,

You've grafted me into Your family.
You've given me new life
through Your love.
Tend my soul today
with Your tender care.
Prune me so I can grow and abound
with Your life-giving fruit.

I invite You to speak to me,
to search my heart and shape my life.
Show me what is right.

Open my eyes to see You.
Open my ears to hear Your voice.
Open my heart to receive Your Word.
Open my hands to accept whatever
*   You give.*

Draw close to me, Lord,
as I draw close to You.

Amen.

Read & Meditate

Read through the Bible passage three times, taking time to pause and pray and quietly listen to the Holy Spirit speaking to your heart.

LECTIO 1: READ THROUGH THE PASSAGE SLOWLY.

What is one word or phrase that stands out to you?

PAUSE & PRAY

In silence, meditate on this word or phrase.

LECTIO 2: READ THROUGH THE PASSAGE A SECOND TIME.

This time, pray through the passage, reading phrase by phrase. Talk to God, pausing to listen and respond to Him as you read.

PAUSE & PRAY

In silence, bring your attention to the present moment.

LECTIO 3: READ THROUGH THE PASSAGE A THIRD TIME.

Sit in stillness again as you contemplate the word or phrase that stood out to you and how it may apply to your life right now.

NOTICE

Notice your body: What are you feeling right now?

Notice your thoughts: What are you thinking right now?

Notice your circumstances: What is happening in your life right now?

Compassionately consider these things, and listen to what the Holy Spirit may be revealing to you in light of today's reading and meditation. What invitation might God be extending to you today?

God is inviting me to . . .

Surrendering Prayer

As I prepare to enter into the rest of my day, Lord,

May Your righteousness and holiness be evident in my life.

May the things that I learn not just be facts that fill my head,
but move them into my heart and out through my hands,
so that my life reflects You in all that I do.

May my pace be slow and unhurried,
ever aware of Your presence with me.

May my mind be attentive and clear,
noticing the gift of every moment.

May my heart be gentle and kind,
showing compassion to myself and others.

Today, I throw off the sin that weighs me down,
and I put on my new nature,
empowered by the Spirit to live like Christ.

Keep turning my thoughts to whatever is right.
Transform me to be more like You.

Amen.

Embody

Continue to contemplate the word and invitation God gave you today.

Consider: What characteristics of the "old nature" have you been hanging on to? What of the "new nature" is evident in your life?

RIGHT LIVING BRINGS JOY

12

PSALM 84:5, 10-12

S cholars believe Psalm 84 was likely penned by David during a time when he was forced away from his home in Jerusalem, either because of his son Absalom's rebellion or because he was away in battle. David lamented being away from the Holy City and God's temple. He expressed his love for God and his desire to be near Him and commune with Him, describing the joy that comes from trusting God and from doing what is right.

At the beginning of this psalm, David longed to make the pilgrimage to Jerusalem, to be in the house of God, to be near Him and worship Him. We, too, are on a lifelong pilgrimage, walking toward the everlasting Holy City of heaven, our eternal home. And God offers us great joy along the way as we follow Him and trust Him. Not that we won't ever enter valleys of weeping or face difficulty or discouragement, but God will be with us through it all and we can trust Him no matter what comes, knowing He will always do what is right and good. After all, as Janet Erskine Stuart so beautifully penned, "Joy is not the absence of suffering, but the presence of God."[16]

Silence

Begin with a time of silence.

Still your body. . . . Slow your breathing. . . . Quiet your mind.

Focus on being fully present in this moment,
right here, right now.

What joy for those whose strength comes from the LORD, who have set their minds on a pilgrimage to Jerusalem. . . .

A single day in your courts is better than a thousand anywhere else! I would rather be a gatekeeper in the house of my God than live the good life in the homes of the wicked. For the LORD God is our sun and our shield. He gives us grace and glory. The LORD will withhold no good thing from those who do what is right. O LORD of Heaven's Armies, what joy for those who trust in you.

PSALM 84:5, 10–12

Opening Prayer

Good and gracious God,

I come to You today just as I am,
with all my failures, all my pain,
all my worries, all my shame—
longing only to be with You.

I invite You to speak to me,
to search my heart and shape my life.
Show me what is right.

Open my eyes to see You.
Open my ears to hear Your voice.
Open my heart to receive Your Word.
Open my hands to accept whatever
     You give.

Draw close to me, Lord,
as I draw close to You.

Amen.

Read & Meditate

Read through the Bible passage three times, taking time to pause and pray and quietly listen to the Holy Spirit speaking to your heart.

LECTIO 1: READ THROUGH THE PASSAGE SLOWLY.
What is one word or phrase that stands out to you?

PAUSE & PRAY
In silence, meditate on this word or phrase.

LECTIO 2: READ THROUGH THE PASSAGE A SECOND TIME.
This time, pray through the passage, reading phrase by phrase.
Talk to God, pausing to listen and respond to Him as you read.

PAUSE & PRAY
In silence, bring your attention to the present moment.

LECTIO 3: READ THROUGH THE PASSAGE A THIRD TIME.
Sit in stillness again as you contemplate the word or phrase that
stood out to you and how it may apply to your life right now.

NOTICE
Notice your body: What are you feeling right now?
Notice your thoughts: What are you thinking right now?
Notice your circumstances: What is happening in your life
right now?

Compassionately consider these things, and listen to what the
Holy Spirit may be revealing to you in light of today's reading and
meditation. What invitation might God be extending to you today?

God is inviting me to . . .

The Lord will withhold no good thing from those who do what is right.

PSALM 84:11

Surrendering Prayer

As I prepare to enter into the rest of my day, Lord,

Strengthen me through Your Word.
You are my strength, my sun, and my shield.
Shine Your light of joy into my life today,
and shield me from the arrows of anxiety that pierce my peace.

May my pace be slow and unhurried,
ever aware of Your presence with me.

May my mind be attentive and clear,
noticing the gift of every moment.

May my heart be gentle and kind,
showing compassion to myself and others.

Today, I give You my worries,
and I receive Your joy and rest.

Keep turning my thoughts to whatever is right.
Transform me to be more like You.

Amen.

Embody

Continue to contemplate the word and invitation God gave you today.

Consider: How many moments of joy can you find today? How can you create some moments of joy today?

....

....

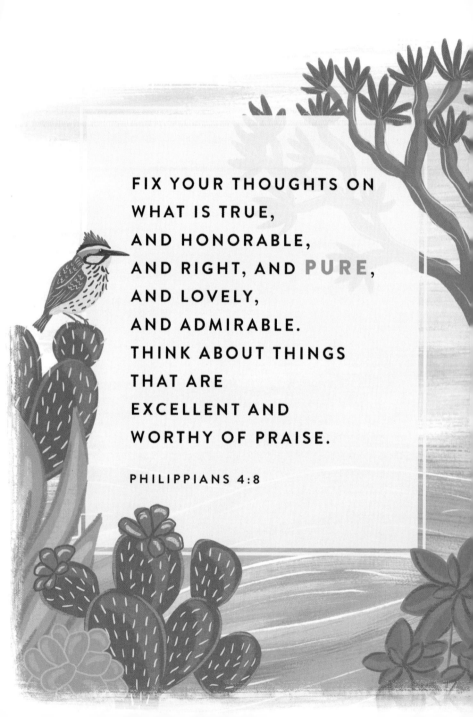

FIX YOUR THOUGHTS ON
WHAT IS TRUE,
AND HONORABLE,
AND RIGHT, AND PURE,
AND LOVELY,
AND ADMIRABLE.
THINK ABOUT THINGS
THAT ARE
EXCELLENT AND
WORTHY OF PRAISE.

PHILIPPIANS 4:8

WHATEVER
IS
pure

WHATEVER IS PURE

The word *pure* means to be "free from dust, dirt, or taint; free from what vitiates [debases], weakens, or pollutes; free from moral fault or guilt."[17] Notice something about that definition? Every phrase begins with the word *free.*

To be pure is to be free. Free from the sin that entangles, from the worry that weighs you down, from the despair that drags you under, from the guilt and shame you carry.

How can we experience this kind of freedom? How do we keep our thoughts fixed on what is pure and live pure lives in this tainted and polluted world? Psalm 119:9 lays it out pretty clearly: "How can a young person stay on the path of purity? By living according to your word" (NIV). Remaining on the path of purity requires aligning your life with God's Word. It means staying on the Way.

If you've ever been on a hike or walked through a thick forest, you've probably been told how important it is to remain on the trail, to not lose sight of the path. This is because it can be very easy to get lost if you don't have something to guide you. It's nearly impossible to walk in a straight line through a forest. Even the smallest shift in direction, barely noticeable at the time, can eventually take you to a drastically different destination.

The only way to know you're still going the right way is if you have a constant and dependable visual landmark or a tool such as a compass.

Without frequently looking at the compass and readjusting your trajectory based on true north, it's very easy to get off track and desperately lost.

It's the same as we walk along the Way with Jesus, as we seek to follow the path of purity with Him. If we don't pay attention to where we're walking, we can get off track pretty easily. We can fall into sin or make moral compromises that veer us off track and send us down paths of impurity and depravity that get us completely lost. A single turn can completely change our destination. God's Word is the daily compass we need to guide us along the Way. When we meditate daily on Scripture, we're intentionally paying attention to the way we're walking and aligning our steps to the Word of God.

Of course, we are all prone to wander, even with daily meditations. We're all tempted at times to take a step off the path, even if just for a moment. That's why staying on the path of purity requires repentance along the way. As we recognize our wandering, we turn back toward Christ and His holy ways. If we want freedom in our pursuit of purity, we need to build repentance into our rhythms. Remaining on the path of purity isn't so much about perfection as it is about direction; it's about staying on the Way and staying close to the One who is perfect and pure. If we do that, we will experience what Jesus said in the Sermon on the Mount: "Blessed are the pure in heart, for they shall see God" (5:8 ESV).

13

THE PATH OF PURITY

PSALM 119·9–16

P salm 119 is the longest chapter in the Bible. The entire psalm declares the greatness of God's Word. There are 176 verses with multiple reiterations of one central, repeating theme: *O Lord, how I love Your law.* The psalmist used twelve different terms (*law, word, statutes, decrees, ordinances,* and the like) more than 180 times to unfold the significance of God's truth.[18] This particular passage focuses on how to remain pure: by learning God's Word, loving God's Word, and living according to God's Word.

As we meditate on this passage, we turn our thoughts toward whatever is pure; we turn our minds toward the path of purity. We consider how the Word of God has the power to purify us—to make us clean and to keep us clean as we turn and return to the pure and holy way of Christ.

Silence

Begin with a time of silence.

Still your body. . . . Slow your breathing. . . . Quiet your mind.

Focus on being fully present in this moment,
right here, right now.

I have hidden your word in my heart that I might not sin against you.

PSALM 119:11 NIV

How can a young person stay on the path of purity? By living according to your word. I seek you with all my heart; do not let me stray from your commands. I have hidden your word in my heart that I might not sin against you. Praise be to you, LORD; teach me your decrees. With my lips I recount all the laws that come from your mouth. I rejoice in following your statutes as one rejoices in great riches. I meditate on your precepts and consider your ways. I delight in your decrees; I will not neglect your word.

PSALM 119:9–16 NIV

Opening Prayer

Heavenly Father,

Still my soul and quiet my mind
so I can hear Your voice today.
Breathe Your peace into me
as I rest in Your presence.

I invite You to speak to me,
to search my heart and shape my life.
Show me what is pure.

Open my eyes to see You.
Open my ears to hear Your voice.
Open my heart to receive Your Word.
Open my hands to accept whatever
*   You give.*

Draw close to me, Lord,
as I draw close to You.

Amen.

Read & Meditate

Read through the Bible passage three times, taking time to pause and pray and quietly listen to the Holy Spirit speaking to your heart.

LECTIO 1: READ THROUGH THE PASSAGE SLOWLY.
What is one word or phrase that stands out to you?

PAUSE & PRAY
In silence, meditate on this word or phrase.

LECTIO 2: READ THROUGH THE PASSAGE A SECOND TIME.
This time, pray through the passage, reading phrase by phrase.
Talk to God, pausing to listen and respond to Him as you read.

PAUSE & PRAY
In silence, bring your attention to the present moment.

LECTIO 3: READ THROUGH THE PASSAGE A THIRD TIME.
Sit in stillness again as you contemplate the word or phrase that
stood out to you and how it may apply to your life right now.

NOTICE
Notice your body: What are you feeling right now?
Notice your thoughts: What are you thinking right now?
Notice your circumstances: What is happening in your life
right now?

Compassionately consider these things, and listen to what the
Holy Spirit may be revealing to you in light of today's reading and
meditation. What invitation might God be extending to you today?

God is inviting me to . . .

Surrendering Prayer

As I prepare to enter into the rest of my day, Lord,

Search my heart with the light of Your love.
Clear away the cobwebs of apathy.
Reveal sins hidden beneath the dust of denial.
Write Your Word in every corner of my heart,
and help me walk on the path of purity.

May my pace be slow and unhurried,
ever aware of Your presence with me.

May my mind be attentive and clear,
noticing the gift of every moment.

May my heart be gentle and kind,
showing compassion to myself and others.

Today, I confess my sins and lay down my shame.
I will rest in Your loving grace and forgiveness.

Keep turning my thoughts to whatever is pure.
Transform me to be more like You.

Amen.

Embody

Continue to contemplate the word and invitation God gave you today.

Consider: What do you need to confess to God? What verse or phrase from Psalm 119 can you tuck into your heart to help you "stay on the path of purity"?

PURIFIED BY TRIALS

14

1 PETER 1:6-7, 13-16

When Peter wrote this letter, the community he was addressing was facing trials so difficult that they were tempted to hopelessness and despair. Peter encouraged them to see not just with physical eyes but to recognize with spiritual eyes that more was happening than they could perceive—a greater truth was unfolding as they were being purified by those circumstances. As the heat of a fire purifies gold by bringing the impurities to the top so they can be removed, trials have a way of purifying our hearts if we let them.

This is not to say that the effects of trauma or tragedy should be minimized or ignored. The burns from some fires leave lasting scars and may require some help to heal. But we are not alone, and we don't have to be afraid when difficulties and discouragement press in. We can shift our focus, turning our thoughts to these truths: we are known by God and have been chosen by God (v. 1); we have been cleansed by the blood of Jesus (v. 2); we have a priceless inheritance through Christ (v. 4); and absolutely nothing can take away our salvation because it is God Himself who is protecting us (v. 5).

Our trials are not the end of the story. We can come through the fire of trial refined—able to live in purity and pursue holiness.

Silence

Begin with a time of silence.

Still your body. . . . Slow your breathing. . . . Quiet your mind.

Focus on being fully present in this moment,
right here, right now.

There is wonderful joy ahead, even though you must endure many trials for a little while. These trials will show that your faith is genuine. It is being tested as fire tests and purifies gold—though your faith is far more precious than mere gold. . . .

So prepare your minds for action and exercise self-control. Put all your hope in the gracious salvation that will come to you when Jesus Christ is revealed to the world. So you must live as God's obedient children. Don't slip back into your old ways of living to satisfy your own desires. You didn't know any better then. But now you must be holy in everything you do, just as God who chose you is holy. For the Scriptures say, "You must be holy because I am holy."

1 PETER 1:6–7, 13–16

Opening Prayer

My God who hears my prayers,

The noise of this world and the weight of my worries make it hard to hear
    Your voice.
So I give all my cares and concerns to You.
Center my heart and mind on You alone.

I invite You to speak to me,
to search my heart and shape my life.
Show me what is pure.

Open my eyes to see You.
Open my ears to hear Your voice.
Open my heart to receive Your Word.
Open my hands to accept whatever
    You give.

Draw close to me, Lord,
as I draw close to You.

Amen.

Read & Meditate

Read through the Bible passage three times, taking time to pause and pray and quietly listen to the Holy Spirit speaking to your heart.

LECTIO 1: READ THROUGH THE PASSAGE SLOWLY.
What is one word or phrase that stands out to you?

PAUSE & PRAY
In silence, meditate on this word or phrase.

LECTIO 2: READ THROUGH THE PASSAGE A SECOND TIME.
This time, pray through the passage, reading phrase by phrase.
Talk to God, pausing to listen and respond to Him as you read.

PAUSE & PRAY
In silence, bring your attention to the present moment.

LECTIO 3: READ THROUGH THE PASSAGE A THIRD TIME.
Sit in stillness again as you contemplate the word or phrase that
stood out to you and how it may apply to your life right now.

NOTICE
Notice your body: What are you feeling right now?
Notice your thoughts: What are you thinking right now?
Notice your circumstances: What is happening in your life
right now?

Compassionately consider these things, and listen to what the
Holy Spirit may be revealing to you in light of today's reading and
meditation. What invitation might God be extending to you today?

God is inviting me to . . .

"BE HOLY

because

I AM HOLY."

1 PETER 1:16

Surrendering Prayer

As I prepare to enter into the rest of my day, Lord,

Purify my heart and mind
as I continue to contemplate Your Word.
In Your way and in rhythm with Your will,
transform my life from the inside out.

May my pace be slow and unhurried,
ever aware of Your presence with me.

May my mind be attentive and clear,
noticing the gift of every moment.

May my heart be gentle and kind,
showing compassion to myself and others.

Today, I give You my troubles and trust You in my trials;
work in my heart and strengthen my faith.

Keep turning my thoughts to whatever is pure.
Transform me to be more like You.

Amen.

Embody

Continue to contemplate the word and invitation God gave you today.

Consider: What trials are you facing that are testing your faith? What is one practical way you can keep your faith strong through the hard days?

15

PURIFIED FROM SIN

PSALM 51:1-4, 7-10

Psalm 51 is one of seven Penitential Psalms. It is a psalm of lament, a heartfelt cry written by David after he was confronted by Nathan about his unspeakable sin with Bathsheba (2 Samuel 11–12). The details of his sin are not laid out here, but David's sincere repentance is evident. He went to God for forgiveness, not because he deserved it but because of his faith in who God was. God's character, not David's own willpower or strength, formed the foundation of his plea. He dared to hope and trust that God would be "merciful and gracious, slow to anger, and abounding in steadfast love and faithfulness, keeping steadfast love for thousands, forgiving iniquity and transgression and sin" (Exodus 34:6–7 ESV).

The purifying work of forgiveness is the work of God alone. We cannot clean our own hearts; only God in His great mercy and steadfast love can do that. But our personal repentance—turning away from sin and toward God—is the doorway to receive that forgiveness. And on the other side of that door is the best surprise: joy!

Silence

Begin with a time of silence.

Still your body.... Slow your breathing.... Quiet your mind.

Focus on being fully present in this moment,
right here, right now.

Because of your great compassion, blot out the stain of my sins.

PSALM 51:1

*Have mercy on me, O God,
because of your unfailing
love. Because of your great
compassion, blot out the stain
of my sins. Wash me clean
from my guilt.
Purify me from my sin.
For I recognize my rebellion;
it haunts me day and night.
Against you, and you alone,
have I sinned; I have done
what is evil in your sight. . . .*

*Purify me from my sins,
and I will be clean;
wash me, and I will be
whiter than snow.
Oh, give me back my joy
again; you have broken me—
now let me rejoice. Don't keep
looking at my sins. Remove
the stain of my guilt.
Create in me a clean heart,
O God. Renew a loyal spirit
within me.*

PSALM 51:1–4, 7–10

Opening Prayer

Forgiving and merciful God,

*My faith in You is so imperfect.
I stumble and waver and doubt.
But You are patient and full of mercy.
Your love for me never ends.*

*I invite You to speak to me,
to search my heart and shape my life.
Show me what is pure.*

*Open my eyes to see You.
Open my ears to hear Your voice.
Open my heart to receive Your Word.
Open my hands to accept whatever
    You give.*

*Draw close to me, Lord,
as I draw close to You.*

Amen.

Read & Meditate

Read through the Bible passage three times, taking time to pause and pray and quietly listen to the Holy Spirit speaking to your heart.

LECTIO 1: READ THROUGH THE PASSAGE SLOWLY.
What is one word or phrase that stands out to you?

PAUSE & PRAY
In silence, meditate on this word or phrase.

LECTIO 2: READ THROUGH THE PASSAGE A SECOND TIME.
This time, pray through the passage, reading phrase by phrase.
Talk to God, pausing to listen and respond to Him as you read.

PAUSE & PRAY
In silence, bring your attention to the present moment.

LECTIO 3: READ THROUGH THE PASSAGE A THIRD TIME.
Sit in stillness again as you contemplate the word or phrase that
stood out to you and how it may apply to your life right now.

NOTICE
Notice your body: What are you feeling right now?
Notice your thoughts: What are you thinking right now?
Notice your circumstances: What is happening in your life
right now?

Compassionately consider these things, and listen to what the
Holy Spirit may be revealing to you in light of today's reading and
meditation. What invitation might God be extending to you today?

God is inviting me to . . .

Surrendering Prayer

As I prepare to enter into the rest of my day, Lord,

May my pace be slow and unhurried,
ever aware of Your presence with me.

May my mind be attentive and clear,
noticing the gift of every moment.

May my heart be gentle and kind,
showing compassion to myself and others.

I am bowed low in humble gratitude because
Your grace displaces my burdens,
Your mercy removes my guilt, and
Your love replaces my shame.

Today, I confess my sins and turn from them;
wash me clean with Your love.

Keep turning my thoughts to whatever is pure.
Transform me to be more like You.

Amen.

Embody

Continue to contemplate the word and invitation God gave you today.

Consider: Has a current circumstance or a past mistake weighed you down with guilt or shame? What can you do today to release that stronghold and accept God's forgiveness and joy instead?

PURE LIVING REFLECTS WISDOM

16

JAMES 3:13-14, 17-18

The pursuit of purity is not about perfection—it's about abiding in Christ, who is perfect. It's about turning and returning to Him, to His wisdom and His ways.

In this passage, James confronted various sins that had become a problem among this community of believers (primarily selfishness, jealousy, fights, and harmful speech), and he called them to repentance, reminding them of a better way.

James contrasted two kinds of wisdom here: false wisdom and true wisdom, the wisdom of the world and the wisdom of God. Worldly wisdom puts self at the center, leading to jealousy, pride, selfishness, and quarrelsomeness. In contrast, godly wisdom puts Christ at the center, which leads to humility, mercy, gentleness, peacefulness, sincerity, love, and unity.

Once again we are reminded that we are known by our fruit. The kind of wisdom we pursue will be evident in the fruit we produce. If we want to pursue lives of purity, we must seek out this "wisdom from above" (v. 17). And if we face circumstances that challenge our purity, we can ask for help. James wrote: "If you need wisdom, ask our generous God, and he will give it to you" (1:5).

Silence

Begin with a time of silence.

Still your body. . . . Slow your breathing. . . . Quiet your mind.

Focus on being fully present in this moment, right here, right now.

If you are wise and understand God's ways, prove it by living an honorable life, doing good works with the humility that comes from wisdom. But if you are bitterly jealous and there is selfish ambition in your heart, don't cover up the truth with boasting and lying. . . .

The wisdom from above is first of all pure. It is also peace loving, gentle at all times, and willing to yield to others. It is full of mercy and the fruit of good deeds. It shows no favoritism and is always sincere. And those who are peacemakers will plant seeds of peace and reap a harvest of righteousness.

JAMES 3:13–14, 17–18

Opening Prayer

Pure and holy Lord,

Calm my mind and settle my thoughts.
Help me to not be overcome by
ruminations on the past
or worries about the future
but to simply rest in gratitude
in this present moment.

I invite You to speak to me,
to search my heart and shape my life.
Show me what is pure.

Open my eyes to see You.
Open my ears to hear Your voice.
Open my heart to receive Your Word.
Open my hands to accept whatever
     You give.

Draw close to me, Lord,
as I draw close to You.

Amen.

Read & Meditate

Read through the Bible passage three times, taking time to pause and pray and quietly listen to the Holy Spirit speaking to your heart.

LECTIO 1: READ THROUGH THE PASSAGE SLOWLY.
What is one word or phrase that stands out to you?

> **PAUSE & PRAY**
> In silence, meditate on this word or phrase.

LECTIO 2: READ THROUGH THE PASSAGE A SECOND TIME.
This time, pray through the passage, reading phrase by phrase.
Talk to God, pausing to listen and respond to Him as you read.

> **PAUSE & PRAY**
> In silence, bring your attention to the present moment.

LECTIO 3: READ THROUGH THE PASSAGE A THIRD TIME.
Sit in stillness again as you contemplate the word or phrase that
stood out to you and how it may apply to your life right now.

> **NOTICE**
> Notice your body: What are you feeling right now?
> Notice your thoughts: What are you thinking right now?
> Notice your circumstances: What is happening in your life
> right now?

Compassionately consider these things, and listen to what the
Holy Spirit may be revealing to you in light of today's reading and
meditation. What invitation might God be extending to you today?

God is inviting me to . . .

THE WISDOM FROM ABOVE

IS FIRST OF ALL

pure.

JAMES 3:17

Surrendering Prayer

As I prepare to enter into the rest of my day, Lord,

May my pace be slow and unhurried,
ever aware of Your presence with me.

May my mind be attentive and clear,
noticing the gift of every moment.

May my heart be gentle and kind,
showing compassion to myself and others.

May Your wisdom be evident in me:
pure and peace loving, gentle at all times,
willing to yield to others, and
full of mercy and the fruit of good deeds.

Today, I will uproot any selfishness or jealousy within me
and plant seeds of peace wherever I go.

Keep turning my thoughts to whatever is pure.
Transform me to be more like You.

Amen.

Embody

Continue to contemplate the word and invitation God gave you today.

Consider: Do you seek godly wisdom in your life, or are you drawn to what the world says is best? Ask God for wisdom in a challenging situation where it might be tempting to compromise.

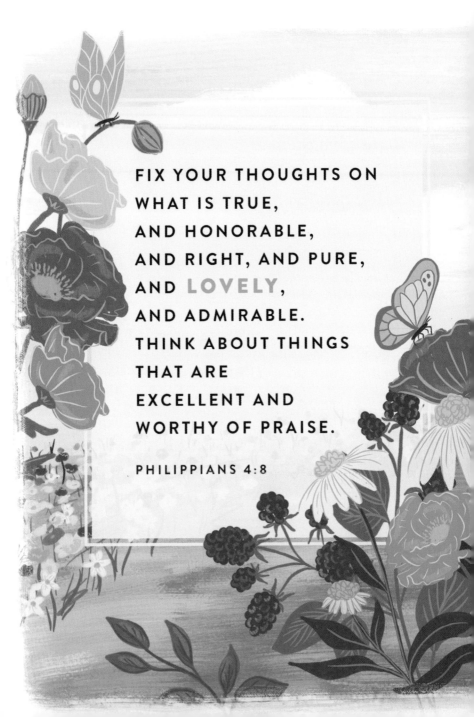

FIX YOUR THOUGHTS ON
WHAT IS TRUE,
AND HONORABLE,
AND RIGHT, AND PURE,
AND LOVELY,
AND ADMIRABLE.
THINK ABOUT THINGS
THAT ARE
EXCELLENT AND
WORTHY OF PRAISE.

PHILIPPIANS 4:8

WHATEVER
IS
lovely

WHATEVER IS LOVELY

What comes to mind when you think of the word *lovely*? What would you describe as being lovely? The dictionary defines it as "delightful for beauty, harmony, or grace."[19] One Bible commentator pointed out that it is used in Philippians 4:8 to mean "that which calls forth love, love-inspiring."[20]

So when we think about "whatever is lovely," we turn our thoughts toward things that inspire us to *love*. We think about things that reflect beauty and grace; we meditate on ideas that inspire unity and peace; and we contemplate things that will increase our love for God, our kindness toward others, and our compassion toward ourselves.

You can think about all that is lovely in the world. God has filled the entire planet with so much beauty and wonder. From the stars in the sky to the beetles on the ground, from the way the leaves rustle in the wind to how the grass feels beneath our toes—all of creation is full of beautiful, inspiring details. Take time to notice the expressions of God's love all around you in the world He created. Think on these things with delight and praise.

You can think about the loveliness of God Himself. God *is* love. It's who He is. And His love is faithful and sure. Nothing you can do will make Him love you any less or any more than He already does. He loves you with a love that is unending and enduring. "Nothing can ever separate us from God's love" (Romans 8:38). What better inspiration is there to love than His great love for us?

When you're feeling unloved or unlovable, turn your thoughts to the truth of God's love for you. His love upholds and enfolds you, right where you are, just as you are. And His love is working in you to keep you turning and returning to Him, reaching to the deepest and darkest corners of your heart and mind, making you clean and whole and new—entirely lovely from the inside out.

You can also think about all that is lovely in the people around you. God's handiwork is on display in the people He created, the crown jewels of His creation. Sometimes it can be challenging to look for the lovely in messy, complicated people—but from the love of God that abides with us and in us through Christ, we get to love one another. We get to see each other as God sees us—lovely, pleasing works of art. There is no greater reflection of Christ in our lives than in the way we see and love one another. When we think on whatever is lovely, we are able to live out of that love-inspiring place, rooted in God's love and overflowing with love to ourselves and others.

17

THE LOVELINESS OF OUR WORLD

PSALM 104:12-14, 16-19, 24

P salm 104 is known as a creation psalm, written to celebrate God's magnificent handiwork. The psalmist uses vibrant imagery and powerful metaphors to paint this picture pointing out the goodness, splendor, complexity, and interrelatedness of all God made. The intricate loveliness of our world reflects God's sovereignty and wisdom in creating and sustaining everything.

This psalm reminds us that the glory of God is manifest all around us in the works of creation, in the rhythmic ordering of the world and all its parts. The sun and moon, seas and rivers, mountains and valleys, animals, birds, fish, and vegetation—all reveal God's wondrous handiwork. The way the birds nest in trees, the rain falls on the fields and makes things grow, and how the plants then nourish the animals— the interconnectedness of His created order is evident. And like a song of joy sung through the movements of the seasons, the whole of creation sings of God's glory and greatness. And what a lovely song it is!

Silence

Begin with a time of silence.

Still your body. . . . Slow your breathing. . . . Quiet your mind.

Focus on being fully present in this moment,
right here, right now.

What a wildly wonderful world, God!

YOU MADE IT ALL,
WITH WISDOM AT YOUR SIDE,
MADE EARTH OVERFLOW
WITH YOUR WONDERFUL
CREATIONS.

PSALM 104:24 MSG

The birds nest beside the streams and sing among the branches of the trees. You send rain on the mountains from your heavenly home, and you fill the earth with the fruit of your labor. You cause grass to grow for the livestock and plants for people to use....

The trees of the LORD are well cared for—the cedars of Lebanon that he planted. There the birds make their nests, and the storks make their homes in the cypresses. High in the mountains live the wild goats, and the rocks form a refuge for the hyraxes. You made the moon to mark the seasons, and the sun knows when to set....

O LORD, what a variety of things you have made!

PSALM 104:12–14, 16–19, 24

Opening Prayer

Glorious creator God,

Your creativity abounds all around me.
All of creation declares Your glory.
Slow me down so I can pay attention;
help me breathe in Your beauty and grace.

I invite You to speak to me,
to search my heart and shape my life.
Show me what is lovely.

Open my eyes to see You.
Open my ears to hear Your voice.
Open my heart to receive Your Word.
Open my hands to accept whatever
*   You give.*

Draw close to me, Lord,
as I draw close to You.

Amen.

Read & Meditate

Read through the Bible passage three times, taking time to pause and pray and quietly listen to the Holy Spirit speaking to your heart.

LECTIO 1: READ THROUGH THE PASSAGE SLOWLY.
What is one word or phrase that stands out to you?

> **PAUSE & PRAY**
> In silence, meditate on this word or phrase.

LECTIO 2: READ THROUGH THE PASSAGE A SECOND TIME.
This time, pray through the passage, reading phrase by phrase.
Talk to God, pausing to listen and respond to Him as you read.

> **PAUSE & PRAY**
> In silence, bring your attention to the present moment.

LECTIO 3: READ THROUGH THE PASSAGE A THIRD TIME.
Sit in stillness again as you contemplate the word or phrase that
stood out to you and how it may apply to your life right now.

> **NOTICE**
> Notice your body: What are you feeling right now?
> Notice your thoughts: What are you thinking right now?
> Notice your circumstances: What is happening in your life
> right now?

Compassionately consider these things, and listen to what the
Holy Spirit may be revealing to you in light of today's reading and
meditation. What invitation might God be extending to you today?

God is inviting me to . . .

Surrendering Prayer

As I prepare to enter into the rest of my day, Lord,

May my pace be slow and unhurried,
ever aware of Your presence with me.

May my mind be attentive and clear,
noticing the gift of every moment.

May my heart be gentle and kind,
showing compassion to myself and others.

May I make space in my day today
to notice the beauty of creation.
Help me breathe in Your peace as I soak in the glory
of the wondrous world around me.

Today, I will quiet the noise and hush the hurry
and let something lovely fill me with wonder.

Keep turning my thoughts to whatever is lovely.
Transform me to be more like You.

Amen.

Embody

Continue to contemplate the word and invitation God gave you today.

Consider: When was the last time you walked through a forest or sat beside a stream or gazed up at the sky? Where can you go today to intentionally look for lovely things in the world around you?

THE LOVELINESS OF OUR LORD

18

PSALM 45:1-7

This psalm is a prophetic psalm about the Messiah. Using imagery from a royal wedding, the psalmist depicts a beautiful picture of the love between Christ and His church. The king is described as a man eternally blessed by God—a mighty warrior of excellent character, more powerful than all the nations. This king is none other than the Messiah, Jesus Christ, God Himself. The royal bride, so beautifully dressed, is a picture of the church—of the collective group of Christ followers all around the world.[21]

Psalm 45 is a beautiful picture of Jesus and gives us so many aspects of the Lord to think about. He is majestic and victorious. He defends truth and justice. He loves what is good, and we are made beautiful by His love. In reading these verses, we turn our hearts to Christ and focus our attention on Him—the fairest, loveliest of all.

Silence

Begin with a time of silence.

Still your body. . . . Slow your breathing. . . . Quiet your mind.

Focus on being fully present in this moment,
right here, right now.

My heart is overflowing with a
beautiful thought! I will write
a lovely poem to the King,
for I am as full of words
as the speediest writer
pouring out his story.
You are the fairest of all;
Your words are filled with grace;
God himself is blessing you
forever. Arm yourself, O mighty
one, so glorious, so majestic!
And in your majesty go on
to victory, defending truth,
humility, and justice.
Go forth to awe-inspiring
deeds! Your arrows are sharp in
your enemies' hearts;
they fall before you.
Your throne, O God, endures
forever. Justice is your royal
scepter. You love what is good
and hate what is wrong.
Therefore God, your God, has
given you more gladness
than anyone else.

PSALM 45:1–7 TLB

Opening Prayer

Beautiful King Jesus,

Your loveliness is beyond words.
Your beautiful grace fills me with joy.
Your remarkable mercy covers my faults.
Your glorious love transforms my heart.

I invite You to speak to me,
to search my heart and shape my life.
Show me what is lovely.

Open my eyes to see You.
Open my ears to hear Your voice.
Open my heart to receive Your Word.
Open my hands to accept whatever
    You give.

Draw close to me, Lord,
as I draw close to You.

Amen.

Read & Meditate

Read through the Bible passage three
times, taking time to pause and pray and
quietly listen to the Holy Spirit speaking
to your heart.

LECTIO 1: READ THROUGH THE PASSAGE SLOWLY.
What is one word or phrase that stands out to you?

PAUSE & PRAY
In silence, meditate on this word or phrase.

LECTIO 2: READ THROUGH THE PASSAGE A SECOND TIME.
This time, pray through the passage, reading phrase by phrase.
Talk to God, pausing to listen and respond to Him as you read.

PAUSE & PRAY
In silence, bring your attention to the present moment.

LECTIO 3: READ THROUGH THE PASSAGE A THIRD TIME.
Sit in stillness again as you contemplate the word or phrase that
stood out to you and how it may apply to your life right now.

NOTICE
Notice your body: What are you feeling right now?
Notice your thoughts: What are you thinking right now?
Notice your circumstances: What is happening in your life
right now?

Compassionately consider these things, and listen to what the
Holy Spirit may be revealing to you in light of today's reading and
meditation. What invitation might God be extending to you today?

God is inviting me to . . .

You are the fairest of all;
your words are filled with grace;
God himself is blessing you forever.

PSALM 45:2 TLB

Surrendering Prayer

As I prepare to enter into the rest of my day, Lord,

May my pace be slow and unhurried,
ever aware of Your presence with me.

May my mind be attentive and clear,
noticing the gift of every moment.

May my heart be gentle and kind,
showing compassion to myself and others.

May I think of You as often as I can today,
remembering Your majesty and beauty and grace.
The riches of a thousand worlds can't compare
to one tiny drop of Your love.

Today, I set aside the distractions,
and I set my eyes on You, resting in Your beautiful, perfect love.

Keep turning my thoughts to whatever is lovely.
Transform me to be more like You.

Amen.

Embody

Continue to contemplate the word and invitation God gave you today.

Consider: What aspect of Jesus do you long to see right now—His power, His grace, His enduring love? How can this affect the way you live?

....

....

19

WE ARE LOVELY WHEN WE LOVE LIKE GOD

1 JOHN 4:7-9, 11-12

John's primary purpose in this letter was to call a divided church to *koinonia* (fellowship) and true unity—the same kind of unity that the Son has enjoyed with the Father from the beginning, a unity defined by love. This appeal for *koinonia* centers on the one attribute of God that embodies all others—that God is love. He is the source and definition of love. His love is steadier and more certain than the ground we walk on. It is unearned, undeserved, and completely free. There's nothing we can do to earn it and nothing we can do to lose it. We are loved. We are His beloved. Period.

God's love was made real and present through Jesus, through His life and His atoning sacrifice for us. His love continues through the life-giving presence of the Holy Spirit with us. The more fully we know God and His love, the more we will overflow with God's love to others. We are most like Jesus—the loveliest of all—when we love as He loves.

Silence

Begin with a time of silence.

Still your body. . . . Slow your breathing. . . . Quiet your mind.

Focus on being fully present in this moment,
right here, right now.

If we love
one another,
God dwells
deeply
within us.

1 JOHN 4:12 MSG

Let us continue to love each other since love comes from God. Everyone who loves is born of God and experiences a relationship with God. The person who refuses to love doesn't know the first thing about God, because God is love—so you can't know him if you don't love. This is how God showed his love for us: God sent his only Son into the world so we might live through him. . . .

If God loved us like this, we certainly ought to love each other. No one has seen God, ever. But if we love one another, God dwells deeply within us, and his love becomes complete in us—perfect love!

1 JOHN 4:7–9, 11–12 MSG

Opening Prayer

Life-giving God of love,

The more I know You, the more I love You.
The more I am with You,
the nearer I want to be.
I want to sit at Your feet today
and rest in Your loving presence.

I invite You to speak to me,
to search my heart and shape my life.
Show me what is lovely.

Open my eyes to see You.
Open my ears to hear Your voice.
Open my heart to receive Your Word.
Open my hands to accept whatever
    You give.

Draw close to me, Lord,
as I draw close to You.

Amen.

Read & Meditate

Read through the Bible passage three times, taking time to pause and pray and quietly listen to the Holy Spirit speaking to your heart.

LECTIO 1: READ THROUGH THE PASSAGE SLOWLY.
What is one word or phrase that stands out to you?

> **PAUSE & PRAY**
> In silence, meditate on this word or phrase.

LECTIO 2: READ THROUGH THE PASSAGE A SECOND TIME.
This time, pray through the passage, reading phrase by phrase.
Talk to God, pausing to listen and respond to Him as you read.

> **PAUSE & PRAY**
> In silence, bring your attention to the present moment.

LECTIO 3: READ THROUGH THE PASSAGE A THIRD TIME.
Sit in stillness again as you contemplate the word or phrase that
stood out to you and how it may apply to your life right now.

> **NOTICE**
> Notice your body: What are you feeling right now?
> Notice your thoughts: What are you thinking right now?
> Notice your circumstances: What is happening in your life
> right now?

Compassionately consider these things, and listen to what the
Holy Spirit may be revealing to you in light of today's reading and
meditation. What invitation might God be extending to you today?

God is inviting me to . . .

Surrendering Prayer

As I prepare to enter into the rest of my day, Lord,

May my pace be slow and unhurried,
ever aware of Your presence with me.

May my mind be attentive and clear,
noticing the gift of every moment.

May my heart be gentle and kind,
showing compassion to myself and others.

I know that nothing I do can make You love me any less,
and nothing I do can make You love me any more.
Help me to live rooted and secure in that love
so that I can freely give it to everyone I meet.

Today, I let go of the fear of what people might think,
and I choose to simply love with abandon.

Keep turning my thoughts to whatever is lovely.
Transform me to be more like You.

Amen.

Embody

Continue to contemplate the word and invitation God gave you today.

Consider: How well do you love others, really? As you contemplate this and examine your heart, are there expectations or limits you put on loving people? What is a tangible way you can love someone today?

LOVELY LIVING EMBODIES REAL LOVE

20

1 CORINTHIANS 13:4-7

First Corinthians 13 is often referred to as "the wedding text" because of its focus on love and its use at many wedding celebrations. But it actually isn't about romantic love; it's about love within the Christian community.

Prior to this passage, Paul had been explaining the various spiritual gifts given to believers and how they were to be used to serve one another within the body of Christ. Paul acknowledged that though there were differences within the body, those differences shouldn't divide but rather should work to build unity. He encouraged believers to use their gifts to edify and serve each other but emphasized the most important of these gifts: love. Gifts won't do any good if they aren't used in love.

When we embody God's love, it has the extraordinary power to create, sustain, and build Christian unity. Without it, all of our spiritual gifts are pointless and our good works are useless. Without love, there can be no unity or peace. Without it, we can't be a light to a watching world.

Silence

Begin with a time of silence.

Still your body. . . . Slow your breathing. . . . Quiet your mind.

Focus on being fully present in this moment,
right here, right now.

*Love is patient and kind.
Love is not jealous or boastful
or proud or rude. It does not
demand its own way. It is not
irritable, and it keeps no record
of being wronged. It does not
rejoice about injustice but
rejoices whenever the truth
wins out. Love never gives up,
never loses faith, is always
hopeful, and endures through
every circumstance.*

1 CORINTHIANS 13:4–7

Opening Prayer

Author and Sustainer of my soul,

*I set aside the things of this world
and the worries of my life right now.
I want to rest in Your love for me today,
wrapped in the warmth
of Your gentle care.*

*I invite You to speak to me,
to search my heart and shape my life.
Show me what is lovely.*

*Open my eyes to see You.
Open my ears to hear Your voice.
Open my heart to receive Your Word.
Open my hands to accept whatever
You give.*

*Draw close to me, Lord,
as I draw close to You.*

Amen.

Read & Meditate

Read through the Bible passage three
times, taking time to pause and pray and
quietly listen to the Holy Spirit speaking
to your heart.

LECTIO 1: READ THROUGH THE PASSAGE SLOWLY.
What is one word or phrase that stands out to you?

PAUSE & PRAY
In silence, meditate on this word or phrase.

LECTIO 2: READ THROUGH THE PASSAGE A SECOND TIME.
This time, pray through the passage, reading phrase by phrase.
Talk to God, pausing to listen and respond to Him as you read.

PAUSE & PRAY
In silence, bring your attention to the present moment.

LECTIO 3: READ THROUGH THE PASSAGE A THIRD TIME.
Sit in stillness again as you contemplate the word or phrase that
stood out to you and how it may apply to your life right now.

NOTICE
Notice your body: What are you feeling right now?
Notice your thoughts: What are you thinking right now?
Notice your circumstances: What is happening in your life
right now?

Compassionately consider these things, and listen to what the
Holy Spirit may be revealing to you in light of today's reading and
meditation. What invitation might God be extending to you today?

God is inviting me to . . .

NEVER GIVES UP,
NEVER LOSES FAITH,
IS ALWAYS HOPEFUL,
AND ENDURES
THROUGH EVERY
CIRCUMSTANCE.

1 CORINTHIANS 13:7

Surrendering Prayer

As I prepare to enter into the rest of my day, Lord,

May my pace be slow and unhurried,
ever aware of Your presence with me.

May my mind be attentive and clear,
noticing the gift of every moment.

May my heart be gentle and kind,
showing compassion to myself and others.

You have loved me with an everlasting love,
a love that cannot be hidden or hoarded
but must be lived and shared and given away.

Today, I will give You my insecurities and fears,
and I will walk boldly in Your love.

Keep turning my thoughts to whatever is lovely.
Transform me to be more like You.

Amen.

Embody

Continue to contemplate the word and invitation God gave you today.

Consider: What part of this passage is hardest for you to embody? Whom can you love with a 1 Corinthians 13 kind of love today?

....

....

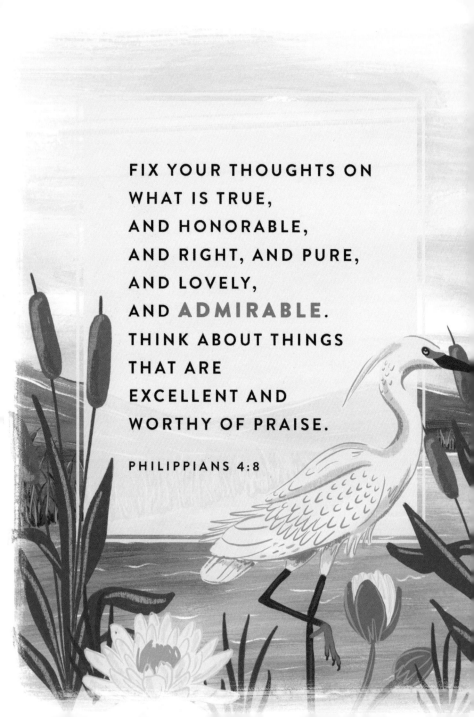

FIX YOUR THOUGHTS ON
WHAT IS TRUE,
AND HONORABLE,
AND RIGHT, AND PURE,
AND LOVELY,
AND **ADMIRABLE**.
THINK ABOUT THINGS
THAT ARE
EXCELLENT AND
WORTHY OF PRAISE.

PHILIPPIANS 4:8

WHATEVER

IS

admirable

WHATEVER IS ADMIRABLE

The word admirable has roots in the Latin word *admirabilis*, "to be wondered at,"[22] and means "deserving the highest esteem"[23] and "deserving respect and approval."[24] Some Bible versions translate this word in Philippians 4:8 as "of good report," or "commendable." When you think about someone you admire or look up to, what commendable qualities or character traits do you consider admirable? Maybe it's honesty, integrity, confidence, faithfulness, trustworthiness, or compassion. Whatever the qualities, when we think of "whatever is admirable," it ultimately draws us to God Himself, who is most worthy of our deepest admiration.

In a fallen world wracked with brokenness and sin, it's easy to become discouraged by all that isn't as it should be. It can be easier to see what is contemptible—lying, stealing, cheating, hypocrisy, judgmentalism, selfishness, unrighteous anger, a lack of forgiveness—than what is commendable. And if we're honest, we can see those contemptible things in ourselves too. None of us is entirely admirable or commendable in all our ways.

It's good to meditate on and look for admirable qualities in ourselves and in others, especially when they reflect the heart and character of Christ. The meditations in this section look at some biblical figures who displayed admirable qualities worth our attention. We see admirable faith in Shadrach, Meshach, and Abednego (Daniel 3). We see admirable courage in King Jehoshaphat (2 Chronicles 20). We see admirable attention to Christ in Mary and Martha (Luke 10). And, of course, Christ and His admirable qualities are worth our supreme focus, as we seek to imitate Him as we grow in faith (Philippians 2).

In our everyday lives, it may be easier to notice the big acts of bravery or generosity, like when a firefighter rushes into a burning building to save someone trapped inside or when an anonymous donor provides trucks full of Christmas presents for families in need. These are the big things that make headlines, the feel-good stories that are intended to inspire admiration in all who hear.

But if we train our eyes to look for what is admirable in the smaller, nearby places, we'll begin to see echoes of God's goodness all around us every day. We'll see kindness in the smile of the bagger at the grocery store; we'll notice joyfulness in the child skipping down the sidewalk; we'll see patience in the mother making her way through the store with three kids in tow; and we'll notice faithfulness in the friend who answers the phone when we call.

When we look for what is admirable, we find evidence of God's compassion and grace, reflections of His redemptive work all over the world—sometimes in the most unexpected places and the most unlikely people. Even, miraculously, within ourselves. God is at work in us and through us to bring His love and redemption into the world. And we get to participate in this work as we seek out and live out the admirable qualities that reflect His heart.

21

ADMIRABLE FAITH

DANIEL 3:1-30

The story of Shadrach, Meshach, and Abednego is part of a larger series of stories in Daniel 1-6 that deal with the relationship between the God of Israel and the gentile kings.

In this chapter, Nebuchadnezzar, the Babylonian king, had erected a massive golden statue. It stood ninety feet tall and nine feet wide, likely created in honor of Nabu, the patron god of Nebuchadnezzar. The king demanded that everyone in the kingdom bow down to the statue and proclaim allegiance. Anyone who disobeyed would be thrown into a blazing furnace (v. 6).

The Jews in the kingdom would not submit to this decree, however. Three friends, Shadrach, Meshach, and Abednego, were quickly singled out and brought before the king. Nebuchadnezzar was furious. He gave them one more chance to bow down and worship and warned that they would be thrown into the furnace if they didn't. "What god will be able to rescue you from my power?" (v. 15). The conflict was between the kingship of Nebuchadnezzar and the power of God. In the friends' response, we see remarkable, admirable faith.

Silence

Begin with a time of silence.

Still your body. . . . Slow your breathing. . . . Quiet your mind.

Focus on being fully present in this moment,
right here, right now.

IF WE ARE THROWN INTO
THE BLAZING FURNACE,
THE GOD WHOM WE SERVE
IS ABLE TO SAVE US.

DANIEL 3:17

Shadrach, Meshach, and
Abednego replied,
"O Nebuchadnezzar, we do not
need to defend ourselves before
you. If we are thrown into the
blazing furnace, the God whom
we serve is able to save us. He
will rescue us from your power,
Your Majesty. But even if he
doesn't . . . we will never serve
your gods or worship the gold
statue you have set up." . . .

So [they], securely tied, fell
into the roaring flames.
But suddenly, Nebuchadnezzar
jumped up in amazement and
exclaimed to his advisers,
"Didn't we tie up three men
and throw them into the
furnace? . . . I see four men,
unbound, walking around in the
fire unharmed! And the fourth
looks like a god!"

DANIEL 3:16–18, 23–25

Opening Prayer

Sovereign Lord,

You alone are the one true God,
full of mercy and infinite love.
You are worthy of my attentive
*   awareness today.*
Help me turn my mind and heart to You.

I invite You to speak to me,
to search my heart and shape my life.
Show me what is admirable.

Open my eyes to see You.
Open my ears to hear Your voice.
Open my heart to receive Your Word.
Open my hands to accept whatever
*   You give.*

Draw close to me, Lord,
as I draw close to You.

Amen.

Read & Meditate

Read through the Bible passage three
times, taking time to pause and pray and
quietly listen to the Holy Spirit speaking
to your heart.

LECTIO 1: READ THROUGH THE PASSAGE SLOWLY.
What is one word or phrase that stands out to you?

PAUSE & PRAY
In silence, meditate on this word or phrase.

LECTIO 2: READ THROUGH THE PASSAGE A SECOND TIME.
This time, pray through the passage, reading phrase by phrase.
Talk to God, pausing to listen and respond to Him as you read.

PAUSE & PRAY
In silence, bring your attention to the present moment.

LECTIO 3: READ THROUGH THE PASSAGE A THIRD TIME.
Sit in stillness again as you contemplate the word or phrase that
stood out to you and how it may apply to your life right now.

NOTICE
Notice your body: What are you feeling right now?
Notice your thoughts: What are you thinking right now?
Notice your circumstances: What is happening in your life
right now?

Compassionately consider these things, and listen to what the
Holy Spirit may be revealing to you in light of today's reading and
meditation. What invitation might God be extending to you today?

God is inviting me to . . .

Surrendering Prayer

As I prepare to enter into the rest of my day, Lord,

May my pace be slow and unhurried,
ever aware of Your presence with me.

May my mind be attentive and clear,
noticing the gift of every moment.

May my heart be gentle and kind,
showing compassion to myself and others.

Make me brave and bold and full of faith in You.
Whatever impossible mountain I face,
whatever difficult choices I must make,
give me courage to do what is right, no matter what.

Today, I give You my fears, and I trust You with my life;
I know You are with me and will never leave me.

Keep turning my thoughts to whatever is admirable.
Transform me to be more like You.

Amen.

Embody

Continue to contemplate the word and invitation God gave you today.

Consider: What fears are keeping you from fully trusting God? What is one small step you can take today to trust God "even if"?

....

....

ADMIRABLE COURAGE

22

2 CHRONICLES 20:1–30

K ing Jehoshaphat was the fourth king of Judah, and in this passage we find him facing several armies from an alliance of nations that were marching against his kingdom. When he was told how close the armies were, Jehoshaphat was alarmed (some translations say "terrified" or "badly shaken") and sought the Lord's help, asking all of Judah to fast (v. 3).

Through a man named Jahaziel, the Lord told Jehoshaphat that He would deliver Judah without a fight. He directed the army to meet the enemy, not to engage in battle, but to "stand still and watch the LORD's victory" (vv. 14–17). So Jehoshaphat led his army where God directed them, placing singers on the front lines to lead the way with worship. When they began to sing, the nations' army turned against each other and began to fight each other instead of God's people (vv. 22–23). By the time Jehoshaphat's army reached the lookout point, there was no living enemy left to fight. They had already been defeated.

To seek God and follow Him in the face of such odds and with such overwhelming fear took admirable courage.

Silence

Begin with a time of silence.

Still your body. . . . Slow your breathing. . . . Quiet your mind.

Focus on being fully present in this moment,
right here, right now.

"Our God, will you not judge them? For we have no power to face this vast army that is attacking us. We do not know what to do, but our eyes are on you." . . .

[Jahaziel said:] "This is what the LORD says to you: 'Do not be afraid or discouraged because of this vast army. For the battle is not yours, but God's. . . . You will not have to fight this battle. Take up your positions; stand firm and see the deliverance the LORD will give you, Judah and Jerusalem. Do not be afraid; do not be discouraged. Go out to face them tomorrow, and the LORD will be with you.'" . . .

As they set out, Jehoshaphat stood and said, " . . . Have faith in the Lord your God and you will be upheld."

2 CHRONICLES 20:12, 15, 17, 20 NIV

Opening Prayer

Lord of heaven's armies,

I come to You with an overwhelmed heart.
The mountain in front of me seems
     impassable,
and the battles I face seem impossible.
I need Your help. I turn to You.

I invite You to speak to me,
to search my heart and shape my life.
Show me what is admirable.

Open my eyes to see You.
Open my ears to hear Your voice.
Open my heart to receive Your Word.
Open my hands to accept whatever
     You give.

Draw close to me, Lord,
as I draw close to You.

Amen.

Read & Meditate

Read through the Bible passage three times, taking time to pause and pray and quietly listen to the Holy Spirit speaking to your heart.

LECTIO 1: READ THROUGH THE PASSAGE SLOWLY.
What is one word or phrase that stands out to you?

PAUSE & PRAY
In silence, meditate on this word or phrase.

LECTIO 2: READ THROUGH THE PASSAGE A SECOND TIME.
This time, pray through the passage, reading phrase by phrase.
Talk to God, pausing to listen and respond to Him as you read.

PAUSE & PRAY
In silence, bring your attention to the present moment.

LECTIO 3: READ THROUGH THE PASSAGE A THIRD TIME.
Sit in stillness again as you contemplate the word or phrase that
stood out to you and how it may apply to your life right now.

NOTICE
Notice your body: What are you feeling right now?
Notice your thoughts: What are you thinking right now?
Notice your circumstances: What is happening in your life
right now?

Compassionately consider these things, and listen to what the
Holy Spirit may be revealing to you in light of today's reading and
meditation. What invitation might God be extending to you today?

God is inviting me to . . .

HAVE FAITH
IN THE
LORD your GOD
AND YOU WILL BE
UPHELD.

2 CHRONICLES 20:20 NIV

Surrendering Prayer

As I prepare to enter into the rest of my day, Lord,

May my pace be slow and unhurried,
ever aware of Your presence with me.

May my mind be attentive and clear,
noticing the gift of every moment.

May my heart be gentle and kind,
showing compassion to myself and others.

May my faith be rooted not in my feelings but deep in Your Word.
Help me trust that You are with me, even when I can't feel it.
Help me trust that You love me, even when I doubt it.
Help me trust that You won't leave me, even when shame says I deserve it.

Today, I will let go of my control, and I will simply praise You; I know
that You will help me and not abandon me.

Keep turning my thoughts to whatever is admirable.
Transform me to be more like You.

Amen.

Embody

Continue to contemplate the word and invitation God gave you today.

Consider: Jehoshaphat put a praise team at the front of his army. How can you lead with praise as you face your own hard things? What words of worship can you embrace as you walk into whatever battles lie ahead?

23

ADMIRABLE ATTENTION

LUKE 10:38-42

Mary and Martha were the sisters of Jesus' friend Lazarus. In this passage we are privy to just a small moment in their lives when Jesus and his disciples had stopped at their home. We quickly see that the two women had very different focuses. While Martha was busy working to serve their guests, Mary simply sat at the feet of Jesus and listened to His teaching. Martha was focused on service while Mary was focused on presence. Both were doing good things, but when we consider the attitude and the attention of the heart, Mary chose better.

Hospitality was exceedingly important in the culture of that time, but Martha got lost in distractions and overwhelmed by tasks and grew irritated with Mary. At that time in society, a woman's value was in her service to her family and guests at home. But Mary went against these societal expectations. When Martha confronted Jesus about it, He gently corrected her. Martha's worry and distraction were taking her attention away from being truly present with Him.

Mary's example of attention to Jesus, her priority of receiving God's Word, is admirable.

Silence

Begin with a time of silence.

Still your body. . . . Slow your breathing. . . . Quiet your mind.

Focus on being fully present in this moment,
right here, right now.

"MARTHA, MARTHA,"
THE LORD ANSWERED,
"YOU ARE WORRIED AND UPSET
ABOUT MANY THINGS,
BUT FEW THINGS ARE NEEDED—
OR INDEED ONLY ONE.
MARY HAS CHOSEN WHAT IS
BETTER, AND IT WILL NOT BE
TAKEN AWAY FROM HER."

LUKE 10:41–42 NIV

As Jesus and his disciples were on their way, he came to a village where a woman named Martha opened her home to him. She had a sister called Mary, who sat at the Lord's feet listening to what he said. But Martha was distracted by all the preparations that had to be made. She came to him and asked, "Lord, don't you care that my sister has left me to do the work by myself? Tell her to help me!"

"Martha, Martha," the Lord answered, "you are worried and upset about many things, but few things are needed—or indeed only one. Mary has chosen what is better, and it will not be taken away from her."

LUKE 10:38–42 NIV

Opening Prayer

Ever-present Savior,

*Though storms may swirl and whirl
    around me today,
I choose to turn my attention to You.
When You are near,
no fear can capsize me.
You calm the wind and the waves.*

*I invite You to speak to me,
to search my heart and shape my life.
Show me what is admirable.*

*Open my eyes to see You.
Open my ears to hear Your voice.
Open my heart to receive Your Word.
Open my hands to accept whatever
    You give.*

*Draw close to me, Lord,
as I draw close to You.*

Amen.

Read & Meditate

Read through the Bible passage three times, taking time to pause and pray and quietly listen to the Holy Spirit speaking to your heart.

LECTIO 1: READ THROUGH THE PASSAGE SLOWLY.
What is one word or phrase that stands out to you?

PAUSE & PRAY
In silence, meditate on this word or phrase.

LECTIO 2: READ THROUGH THE PASSAGE A SECOND TIME.
This time, pray through the passage, reading phrase by phrase.
Talk to God, pausing to listen and respond to Him as you read.

PAUSE & PRAY
In silence, bring your attention to the present moment.

LECTIO 3: READ THROUGH THE PASSAGE A THIRD TIME.
Sit in stillness again as you contemplate the word or phrase that
stood out to you and how it may apply to your life right now.

NOTICE
Notice your body: What are you feeling right now?
Notice your thoughts: What are you thinking right now?
Notice your circumstances: What is happening in your life
right now?

Compassionately consider these things, and listen to what the
Holy Spirit may be revealing to you in light of today's reading and
meditation. What invitation might God be extending to you today?

God is inviting me to . . .

Surrendering Prayer

As I prepare to enter into the rest of my day, Lord,

May my pace be slow and unhurried,
ever aware of Your presence with me.

May my mind be attentive and clear,
noticing the gift of every moment.

May my heart be gentle and kind,
showing compassion to myself and others.

Many things vie for my attention,
but One is better than them all.
In all that I do, make me mindful of You.
Whether I serve or sit, whether I work or wait,
may my mind be on You and my joy found in You.

Today, I will set aside the distractions,
and I will sit at Your feet and rest in Your presence.

Keep turning my thoughts to whatever is admirable.
Transform me to be more like You.

Amen.

Embody

Continue to contemplate the word and invitation God gave you today.

Consider: What is taking your attention away from Jesus? What one thing can you do today to slow down your pace? What worry do you need to release?

ADMIRABLE LIVING
IMITATES CHRIST

24

PHILIPPIANS 2:5-11

Paul wrote to the Philippian church while he was
imprisoned. In this letter, he called them to live an
authentic Christian life through personal godly behavior
and unity and service to one another as a community of
believers. He reminded them that they were not alone in
their trials. He urged them to live "worthy of the gospel of
Christ" (1:27 NIV), and he set Christ before them as the prime
example.

Verses 6–11 of Philippians 2 are organized in a poetic
pattern and are often referred to as "the Christ hymn." The
hymn follows a pattern of increasing humiliation followed by
increasing exaltation. Christ suffered, but His suffering and
death were not the end of the story.

Jesus is the One who embodies the gospel and the One
who empowers us to live a life worthy of that gospel. He is
worthy of our admiration and imitation. When we model
our lives on Christ—on His tenderness and compassion, His
unity with the Father, His humility and love—we can truly
live a life worthy of the gospel.

Silence

Begin with a time of silence.

Still your body. . . . Slow your breathing. . . . Quiet your mind.

Focus on being fully present in this moment,
right here, right now.

> You must have the same
> attitude that Christ Jesus
> had. Though he was God,
> he did not think of equality
> with God as something to
> cling to. Instead, he gave
> up his divine privileges; he
> took the humble position
> of a slave and was born as
> a human being. When he
> appeared in human form,
> he humbled himself in
> obedience to God and died a
> criminal's death on a cross.
>
> Therefore, God elevated
> him to the place of highest
> honor and gave him the
> name above all other names,
> that at the name of Jesus
> every knee should bow, in
> heaven and on earth and
> under the earth, and every
> tongue declare that Jesus
> Christ is Lord, to the glory
> of God the Father.

PHILIPPIANS 2:5–11

Opening Prayer

Most admirable Jesus,

I come to You in stillness, resting in
     Your grace.
In Your kindness, give me joy.
In Your wisdom, give me strength.
In Your merciful love, give me peace.

I invite You to speak to me,
to search my heart and shape my life.
Show me what is admirable.

Open my eyes to see You.
Open my ears to hear Your voice.
Open my heart to receive Your Word.
Open my hands to accept whatever
     You give.

Draw close to me, Lord,
as I draw close to You.

Amen.

Read & Meditate

Read through the Bible passage three
times, taking time to pause and pray and
quietly listen to the Holy Spirit speaking
to your heart.

LECTIO 1: READ THROUGH THE PASSAGE SLOWLY.
What is one word or phrase that stands out to you?

PAUSE & PRAY
In silence, meditate on this word or phrase.

LECTIO 2: READ THROUGH THE PASSAGE A SECOND TIME.
This time, pray through the passage, reading phrase by phrase.
Talk to God, pausing to listen and respond to Him as you read.

PAUSE & PRAY
In silence, bring your attention to the present moment.

LECTIO 3: READ THROUGH THE PASSAGE A THIRD TIME.
Sit in stillness again as you contemplate the word or phrase that
stood out to you and how it may apply to your life right now.

NOTICE
Notice your body: What are you feeling right now?
Notice your thoughts: What are you thinking right now?
Notice your circumstances: What is happening in your life
right now?

Compassionately consider these things, and listen to what the
Holy Spirit may be revealing to you in light of today's reading and
meditation. What invitation might God be extending to you today?

God is inviting me to . . .

You must have
the same attitude
that Christ Jesus had.

PHILIPPIANS 2:5

Surrendering Prayer

As I prepare to enter into the rest of my day, Lord,

May my pace be slow and unhurried,
ever aware of Your presence with me.

May my mind be attentive and clear,
noticing the gift of every moment.

May my heart be gentle and kind,
showing compassion to myself and others.

May my life imitate You today.
With my breath, may I praise You.
With my heart, may I trust You.
With my mind, may I honor You.
With my hands, may I serve You.

Today, may everything I do and say be seasoned
with kindness and goodness and grace.

Keep turning my thoughts to whatever is admirable.
Transform me to be more like You.

Amen.

Embody

Continue to contemplate the word and invitation God gave you today.

Consider: Is selfishness or pride tainting your attitude toward others?
What one tangible thing can you do to imitate Christ?

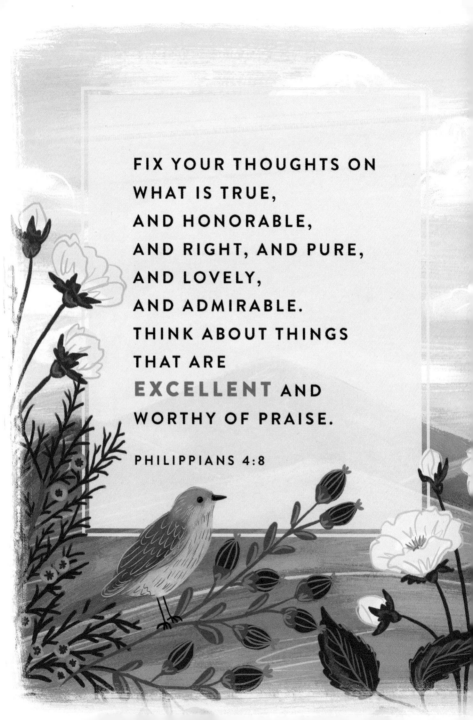

FIX YOUR THOUGHTS ON
WHAT IS TRUE,
AND HONORABLE,
AND RIGHT, AND PURE,
AND LOVELY,
AND ADMIRABLE.
THINK ABOUT THINGS
THAT ARE
EXCELLENT AND
WORTHY OF PRAISE.

PHILIPPIANS 4:8

WHATEVER
IS
excellent

WHATEVER IS EXCELLENT

What is excellent? The dictionary defines *excellent* as "possessing outstanding quality or superior merit; remarkably good; extraordinary; superior."[25]

We usually consider things to be excellent when they surpass our expectations or exceed a common standard. We may describe a delicious meal, an especially entertaining movie, or even a skillfully executed piece of art as excellent. Similarly, kids who make straight A's on their report cards are told they have excellent scores, meaning they scored well above average, exceeding scholastic expectations.

We're often encouraged to strive for excellence in our lives, to do our best to excel in all the ways. We might feel we need to be an excellent employee, the ideal parent, a perfect friend, or the best church member possible. And while I think there can be benefits to this striving, for some of us (I'm looking right at us anxious perfectionists), this can set us up for some pretty unrealistic expectations and inevitable feelings of shame or disappointment when we can't perfectly live up to such a high standard. We become so focused on excelling that we lose sight of what it means to *be* excellent, and we measure our performance, even in spiritual spaces, against the standard of absolute perfection.

The kind of excellence Paul spoke of in Philippians 4—the kind that should fill our minds and hearts—is not an obsession with perfect performance but rather a commitment to consistency of character.

Excellence here has to do with moral virtue and how we reflect the excellent character of Christ. It's not about what we do so much as who we are and, even more so, who God is.

God Himself is excellent in every way. He is far superior to us: "As the heavens are higher than the earth, so are my ways higher than your ways" (Isaiah 55:9 NIV). He is remarkably good: "For the LORD is good. His unfailing love continues forever, and his faithfulness continues to each generation" (Psalm 100:5). He is extraordinary: "The LORD your God is among you, and he is a great and awesome God" (Deuteronomy 7:21). He is our ultimate standard and our source of excellence. When we think about whatever is excellent, we can think about God and all His excellent ways and then attune the ears of our hearts to hear the echoes of His excellence around us and within us.

The more we think about Him and the more we connect our hearts to Him, the more we reflect His presence in our lives, and echo His excellence.

But remember: perfection isn't the goal; presence is. We do not need to obsess over perfect performance. We simply commit to consistent character as we are mindful of our thoughts, turning and returning our minds to whatever is excellent.

25

THE EXCELLENT WAY OF GOD

PSALM 18:30-36

I n this psalm, David recounted all the great things God had done for him. His gratitude overflowed into a litany of praise. God had been his Rock, fortress, shield, and Savior. He had given David protection from enemies, answers to his prayers, and strength to endure. He had steadied his feet, straightened his path, and lightened his darkness.

It's no secret that David was far from perfect. He messed up and sinned in pretty major ways, but he also strove to remain obedient and faithful with God as his refuge and strength. Through sickness and attacks, distress and discouragement, David kept turning his attention to God, remembering the ways God loved and delighted in him. This act of recounting God's mercy and goodness helped David recognize God's faithfulness and remain on His path.

This act of remembering, of turning and returning our thoughts to all the excellent ways of God, remains a valuable practice for us today, helping us notice how God is working and moving in our lives, and giving us courage to keep trusting in His faithful love to keep walking in His perfect way.

Silence

Begin with a time of silence.

Still your body. . . . Slow your breathing. . . . Quiet your mind.

Focus on being fully present in this moment,
right here, right now.

He makes me as
Surefooted as a deer,
enabling me to stand on
mountain heights.

PSALM 18:33

God's way is perfect.
All the LORD's promises prove
true. He is a shield for all who
look to him for protection. For
who is God except the LORD?
Who but our God is a solid
rock? God arms me with
strength, and he makes my
way perfect. He makes me as
surefooted as a deer, enabling
me to stand on mountain
heights. He trains my hands for
battle; he strengthens my arm
to draw a bronze bow.

You have given me your shield
of victory. Your right hand
supports me; your help has
made me great. You have made
a wide path for my feet to keep
them from slipping.

PSALM 18:30–36

Opening Prayer

All-sufficient Lord,

As the light of dawn breaks through
*   the darkness,*
may the light of Your love break through
*   my doubts and fears,*
revealing a landscape of grace,
every shadow in the shade of
*   Your presence.*

I invite You to speak to me,
to search my heart and shape my life.
Show me what is excellent.

Open my eyes to see You.
Open my ears to hear Your voice.
Open my heart to receive Your Word.
Open my hands to accept whatever
*   You give.*

Draw close to me, Lord,
as I draw close to You.

Amen.

Read & Meditate

Read through the Bible passage three times, taking time to pause and pray and quietly listen to the Holy Spirit speaking to your heart.

LECTIO 1: READ THROUGH THE PASSAGE SLOWLY.
What is one word or phrase that stands out to you?

PAUSE & PRAY
In silence, meditate on this word or phrase.

LECTIO 2: READ THROUGH THE PASSAGE A SECOND TIME.
This time, pray through the passage, reading phrase by phrase.
Talk to God, pausing to listen and respond to Him as you read.

PAUSE & PRAY
In silence, bring your attention to the present moment.

LECTIO 3: READ THROUGH THE PASSAGE A THIRD TIME.
Sit in stillness again as you contemplate the word or phrase that
stood out to you and how it may apply to your life right now.

NOTICE
Notice your body: What are you feeling right now?
Notice your thoughts: What are you thinking right now?
Notice your circumstances: What is happening in your life
right now?

Compassionately consider these things, and listen to what the
Holy Spirit may be revealing to you in light of today's reading and
meditation. What invitation might God be extending to you today?

God is inviting me to . . .

Surrendering Prayer

As I prepare to enter into the rest of my day, Lord,

May my pace be slow and unhurried,
ever aware of Your presence with me.

May my mind be attentive and clear,
noticing the gift of every moment.

May my heart be gentle and kind,
showing compassion to myself and others.

May I walk in Your Way today,
following You faithfully as my guide.
Make Your Word the foundation of my heart,
a solid rock on which to steady my life.

Today, I give You all my fears,
and I hold tight to Your promises.

Keep turning my thoughts to whatever is excellent.
Transform me to be more like You.

Amen.

Embody

Continue to contemplate the word and invitation God gave you today.

Consider: What is holding you back from fully embracing the way of God? What one doubt or fear can you give to God today?

....

....

LUKE 12:24-28

I n this section of Luke, often known as the "travel narrative," Jesus had been speaking to a growing multitude of people on His way to Jerusalem. Approximately ten chapters detail His journey and all that He taught and did along the way.

In this passage, after addressing the topic of greed and wealth and providing a proper perspective on riches, Jesus turned to His disciples and reminded them that "life is more than food, and your body more than clothing" (12:23). He emphasized that a true and abundant life for believers is not about material possessions, and there is no need to worry about things such as food or clothing, because God provides for our fundamental needs.

Jesus wasn't suggesting that work is unnecessary. He was addressing worry, not laziness. With compassion and grace, He simply reminds us that we don't have to be afraid or worry. Our security is found not in money but in Christ—and He will take excellent care of us.

Silence

Begin with a time of silence.

Still your body. . . . Slow your breathing. . . . Quiet your mind.

Focus on being fully present in this moment,
right here, right now.

"Look at the ravens. They don't plant or harvest or store food in barns, for God feeds them. And you are far more valuable to him than any birds! Can all your worries add a single moment to your life? And if worry can't accomplish a little thing like that, what's the use of worrying over bigger things?

"Look at the lilies and how they grow. They don't work or make their clothing, yet Solomon in all his glory was not dressed as beautifully as they are. And if God cares so wonderfully for flowers that are here today and thrown into the fire tomorrow, he will certainly care for you."

LUKE 12:24–28

Opening Prayer

Maker and Sustainer of all things,

You have given me breath and life and everything I need.
You are good and faithful and always true.
I set aside all that is cluttering my mind and I place my full attention on You.

I invite You to speak to me, to search my heart and shape my life.
Show me what is excellent.

Open my eyes to see You.
Open my ears to hear Your voice.
Open my heart to receive Your Word.
Open my hands to accept whatever You give.

Draw close to me, Lord, as I draw close to You.

Amen.

Read & Meditate

Read through the Bible passage three times, taking time to pause and pray and quietly listen to the Holy Spirit speaking to your heart.

LECTIO 1: READ THROUGH THE PASSAGE SLOWLY.
What is one word or phrase that stands out to you?

PAUSE & PRAY
In silence, meditate on this word or phrase.

LECTIO 2: READ THROUGH THE PASSAGE A SECOND TIME.
This time, pray through the passage, reading phrase by phrase.
Talk to God, pausing to listen and respond to Him as you read.

PAUSE & PRAY
In silence, bring your attention to the present moment.

LECTIO 3: READ THROUGH THE PASSAGE A THIRD TIME.
Sit in stillness again as you contemplate the word or phrase that
stood out to you and how it may apply to your life right now.

NOTICE
Notice your body: What are you feeling right now?
Notice your thoughts: What are you thinking right now?
Notice your circumstances: What is happening in your life
right now?

Compassionately consider these things, and listen to what the
Holy Spirit may be revealing to you in light of today's reading and
meditation. What invitation might God be extending to you today?

God is inviting me to . . .

"If God cares
so wonderfully
for flowers that
are here today
and thrown into
the fire tomorrow,
he will certainly
care for you."

LUKE 12:28

Surrendering Prayer

As I prepare to enter into the rest of my day, Lord,

May my pace be slow and unhurried,
ever aware of Your presence with me.

May my mind be attentive and clear,
noticing the gift of every moment.

May my heart be gentle and kind,
showing compassion to myself and others.

May I not let the ruminations of yesterday
or the worries of tomorrow
rob me of the joy that is here for me today.
In Your presence—right here in this moment—
is real peace.

Today, I lay down my worries and cares.
I trust that You care about me and You will take care of me.

Keep turning my thoughts to whatever is excellent.
Transform me to be more like You.

Amen.

Embody

Continue to contemplate the word and invitation God gave you today.

Consider: What are you worrying about right now? What is one thing you can do today to trade that worry for trust?

....

....

27   THE EXCELLENT HOPE OF GOD

LAMENTATIONS 3:19–26

The book of Lamentations was written by and for people who had suffered unimaginable trauma. The Babylonians had torn down the walls of their city, knocked down their homes, burned down the temple, and executed the royal family. Everything they relied on for safety, security, comfort, and even identity had been stripped away.

Trauma can affect us in profound and lasting ways. We might push aside our pain or hide our feelings in an effort to "look on the bright side." Or maybe we feel it is embarrassing or weak to share our suffering. But God never said we should suffer in silence. Lamenting the wrong that was done and expressing the difficult emotions that we feel is important and necessary. Lamentations begs to bear witness to pain, to sit with grief, and to give ourselves time to feel its weight, while also reminding us that there is still hope.

In this passage we find this hope. We see a brave act of remembering truths that transcend, though they do not remove or replace, the weight of suffering. We see people in pain who have written the love of God on their very hearts.

Silence

Begin with a time of silence.

Still your body. . . . Slow your breathing. . . . Quiet your mind.

Focus on being fully present in this moment,
right here, right now.

IT'S A GOOD THING TO

QUIETLY HOPE,

QUIETLY HOPE FOR
HELP FROM GOD.

LAMENTATIONS 3:26 MSG

I'll never forget the trouble, the utter lostness, the taste of ashes, the poison I've swallowed. I remember it all— oh, how well I remember—the feeling of hitting the bottom. But there's one other thing I remember, and remembering, I keep a grip on hope:

GOD's loyal love couldn't have run out, his merciful love couldn't have dried up. They're created new every morning. How great your faithfulness! I'm sticking with GOD (I say it over and over). He's all I've got left.

GOD proves to be good to the man who passionately waits, to the woman who diligently seeks. It's a good thing to quietly hope, quietly hope for help from God.

LAMENTATIONS 3:19–26 MSG

Opening Prayer

God of hope and peace,

I am weary and worn down.
Renew me today with Your Spirit.
Still my anxious mind, and give me peace.
Restore my joy as I turn my thoughts
to You.

I invite You to speak to me,
to search my heart and shape my life.
Show me what is excellent.

Open my eyes to see You.
Open my ears to hear Your voice.
Open my heart to receive Your Word.
Open my hands to accept whatever
You give.

Draw close to me, Lord,
as I draw close to You.

Amen.

Read & Meditate

Read through the Bible passage three times, taking time to pause and pray and quietly listen to the Holy Spirit speaking to your heart.

LECTIO 1: READ THROUGH THE PASSAGE SLOWLY.

What is one word or phrase that stands out to you?

PAUSE & PRAY

In silence, meditate on this word or phrase.

LECTIO 2: READ THROUGH THE PASSAGE A SECOND TIME.

This time, pray through the passage, reading phrase by phrase.
Talk to God, pausing to listen and respond to Him as you read.

PAUSE & PRAY

In silence, bring your attention to the present moment.

LECTIO 3: READ THROUGH THE PASSAGE A THIRD TIME.

Sit in stillness again as you contemplate the word or phrase that
stood out to you and how it may apply to your life right now.

NOTICE

Notice your body: What are you feeling right now?
Notice your thoughts: What are you thinking right now?
Notice your circumstances: What is happening in your life
right now?

Compassionately consider these things, and listen to what the
Holy Spirit may be revealing to you in light of today's reading and
meditation. What invitation might God be extending to you today?

God is inviting me to . . .

Surrendering Prayer

As I prepare to enter into the rest of my day, Lord,

May my pace be slow and unhurried,
ever aware of Your presence with me.

May my mind be attentive and clear,
noticing the gift of every moment.

May my heart be gentle and kind,
showing compassion to myself and others.

Help me remember:
Even when I'm weary of waiting, You never stop working.
When I'm struggling to hold on, You keep holding on to me.
When hope is drowned out by darkness and pain,
You are the Light—and You are always, always with me.

Today, even if the worst comes,
You won't let go of me, and I won't let go of hope.

Keep turning my thoughts to whatever is excellent.
Transform me to be more like You.

Amen.

Embody

Continue to contemplate the word and invitation God gave you today.

Consider: What is the worst thing that could happen today? How can you choose to hope even in the midst of this big worst-case worry?

....

....

"You will call to Me
and Come and pray to Me,
and I will listen to you.
You will Seek Me and
find Me when you
search for Me with
all your heart."

JEREMIAH 29:12–13 HCSB

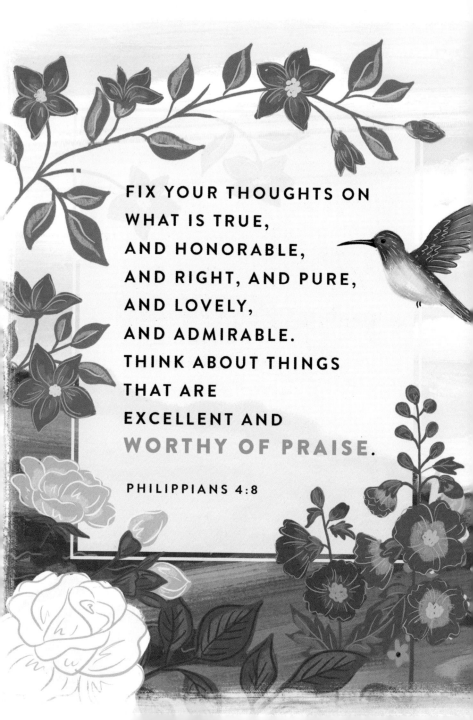

FIX YOUR THOUGHTS ON
WHAT IS TRUE,
AND HONORABLE,
AND RIGHT, AND PURE,
AND LOVELY,
AND ADMIRABLE.
THINK ABOUT THINGS
THAT ARE
EXCELLENT AND
WORTHY OF PRAISE.

PHILIPPIANS 4:8

WHATEVER
IS
worthy
of
praise

WHATEVER IS WORTHY OF PRAISE

I used to have a mixed-up ideology about prayer and praise. In my mind, praise was for the good stuff and prayer was for the hard stuff. I praised God when He answered my prayers (in the way I wanted) and for "blessings" (that made my life easier). My praise was mostly rooted in my circumstances and feelings. After all, it's easy to say "God is good" when good things happen.

But what about when the healing you prayed for doesn't come or when that job you wanted falls through? What about when a friend ghosts you or your spouse leaves or you lose someone you love? How do you praise when you're drowning in the depths of depression or when your mind is flooded with anxiety or when your body is suffering in chronic pain?

While there are a lot of wonderful and beautiful things in our lives that we can and should praise God for, there are many hard and painful things as well. There will be dark and discouraging days, unanswered prayers, unfair circumstances, and seasons of sadness and profound grief. Even then, God is still worthy of our praise.

We praise God not because of our circumstances but because of His character. Genuine praise is dependent not on how we feel but on *who He is*. God is faithful and kind. He is true and just. He is holy and good. He is love, and He loves us with an everlasting love. When we turn our thoughts to whatever is worthy of praise, we turn our thoughts to our loving and faithful God.

We praise Him for what He has done. We remember His promises and all the ways He has been good and faithful and true. We meditate on Scripture to remind us of His love and that He always keeps His promises.

We praise Him for what He is doing. Even when we can't see Him or we don't understand, we can look for the evidence of His goodness right here and now, and we can trust that He is still working and that He wastes nothing.

We praise Him for what is still to come. We trust that He will do all that He said He would do. We know that this small part of our story is not the whole story. We can rest in His love today as we look forward to the future glory and eternal peace He promises.

There is no easy answer to suffering, and our praise does not negate the reality of pain in our world. But praise can transcend even the darkest depths of despair because it reminds us of the reality of God's promises, the dependability of His character, and the certainty of His ultimate victory. So even in the midst of suffering, we can still praise God—because this is how we hold on to hope.

God is great and worthy of our praise, always. He has done great things. And He will keep doing great things. And the greatest things are yet to come.

28

PRAISE GOD FOR ALL HE'S DONE

PSALM 66:1-6, 16-20

P salm 66 begins with a shout, *hari'u*, "an imperative verb meaning: '(Hey, all of you) make some noise! Shout!'"[26] God's awesome deeds deserve a shout of praise—He has done great and mighty things. From the creation of the world and everyday wonders to the rescue of His people and His miraculous resurrection, God has never stopped working His awesome deeds throughout all the earth.

It can be easy to praise in generalities, painting our thanks with a wide brush and saying simply, "Thanks for all You've done." But it's also important to turn our thoughts to specific events where God has provided for us, painting our praise with smaller details of His goodness and grace. In this passage, the psalmist specifically recounts God's deliverance of His people from Egypt by parting the sea and leading them to freedom across the dry land.

Nothing is too hard for God. He's proved it again and again. When we remember what God has done, we gain courage to trust what God will do. When we praise Him for what has been as we wait with hope for what will be, we strengthen our roots of faith and deepen our trust in Him.

Silence

Begin with a time of silence.

Still your body. . . . Slow your breathing. . . . Quiet your mind.

Focus on being fully present in this moment,
right here, right now.

PRAISE GOD,

WHO DID NOT

IGNORE my PRAYER

OR WITHDRAW HIS

UNFAILING LOVE

FROM ME.

PSALM 66:20

Shout joyful praises to God, all the earth! Sing about the glory of his name! Tell the world how glorious he is. Say to God, "How awesome are your deeds! . . .

Everything on earth will worship you; they will sing your praises, shouting your name in glorious songs." . . .

Come and see what our God has done, what awesome miracles he performs for people! He made a dry path through the Red Sea, and his people went across on foot. There we rejoiced in him. . . .

Come and listen, all you who fear God, and I will tell you what he did for me. For I cried out to him for help, praising him as I spoke. If I had not confessed the sin in my heart, the Lord would not have listened. But God did listen! . . . Praise God, who did not ignore my prayer or withdraw his unfailing love from me.

PSALM 66:1–6, 16–20

Opening Prayer

God of all goodness,

You have been so kind to me.
No matter what circumstances
    I am facing,
I know You are with me.
Help me to breathe deeply of Your
    grace today.

I invite You to speak to me,
to search my heart and shape my life.
Show me what is worthy of praise.

Open my eyes to see You.
Open my ears to hear Your voice.
Open my heart to receive Your Word.
Open my hands to accept whatever
    You give.

Draw close to me, Lord,
as I draw close to You.

Amen.

Read & Meditate

Read through the Bible passage three times, taking time to pause and pray and quietly listen to the Holy Spirit speaking to your heart.

What is one word or phrase that stands out to you?

PAUSE & PRAY
In silence, meditate on this word or phrase.

This time, pray through the passage, reading phrase by phrase. Talk to God, pausing to listen and respond to Him as you read.

PAUSE & PRAY
In silence, bring your attention to the present moment.

Sit in stillness again as you contemplate the word or phrase that stood out to you and how it may apply to your life right now.

NOTICE
Notice your body: What are you feeling right now?
Notice your thoughts: What are you thinking right now?
Notice your circumstances: What is happening in your life right now?

Compassionately consider these things, and listen to what the Holy Spirit may be revealing to you in light of today's reading and meditation. What invitation might God be extending to you today?

God is inviting me to . . .

Surrendering Prayer

As I prepare to enter into the rest of my day, Lord,

May my pace be slow and unhurried,
ever aware of Your presence with me.

May my mind be attentive and clear,
noticing the gift of every moment.

May my heart be gentle and kind,
showing compassion to myself and others.

Fill me with praise as I remember Your goodness
and all the ways You've helped me.
May I see the thread of Your faithful love
woven through every moment of my life.

Today, I will interrupt every worry with this truth:
You've been with me through it all, and You are with me still.

Keep turning my thoughts to whatever is worthy of praise.
Transform me to be more like You.

Amen.

Embody

Continue to contemplate the word and invitation God gave you today.

Consider: What specific time in your life can you point to as evidence of God's goodness or help? What can you praise God for today?

PRAISE GOD FOR ALL THAT IS, EVEN THOUGH

29

HABAKKUK 3:17-19

The prophet Habakkuk was called to proclaim God's word to Judah and he spoke honestly to God about his confusion, complaints, and questions. He didn't understand why God hadn't done anything about the rampant sin and corruption in Judah. Where was the justice? Why wasn't He doing anything? God responded that He was coming and He would deal with their sin—but not when or how Habakkuk expected. God's methods and timing are far beyond our understanding. But we can trust that God will always do what He says He will do.

In chapter 3, Habakkuk's pleas and prayers become a psalm. He praises God and recounts how God delivered His people from Egypt and preserved them in their wilderness before leading them into the promised land. He would do it again—but in His way, time, and strength. The road ahead would not be easy, and the battle for Judah would be devastating. Habakkuk could feel his heart pounding as his lips quivered and his body trembled in fear (v. 16). But he didn't question God's ways; instead, he praised God "even though."

Silence

Begin with a time of silence.

Still your body. . . . Slow your breathing. . . . Quiet your mind.

Focus on being fully present in this moment,
right here, right now.

Even though the fig trees have no blossoms, and there are no grapes on the vines; even though the olive crop fails, and the fields lie empty and barren; even though the flocks die in the fields, and the cattle barns are empty, yet I will rejoice in the LORD! I will be joyful in the God of my salvation! The Sovereign LORD is my strength! He makes me as surefooted as a deer, able to tread upon the heights.

HABAKKUK 3:17–19

Opening Prayer

God of my salvation,

My faith feels shaky and unsteady.
I'm blown hard by winds of fear
    and doubt.
Give me strength today to rest in You.
Steady me with Your Word.

I invite You to speak to me,
to search my heart and shape my life.
Show me what is worthy of praise.

Open my eyes to see You.
Open my ears to hear Your voice.
Open my heart to receive Your Word.
Open my hands to accept whatever
    You give.

Draw close to me, Lord,
as I draw close to You.

Amen.

Read & Meditate

Read through the Bible passage three times, taking time to pause and pray and quietly listen to the Holy Spirit speaking to your heart.

LECTIO 1: READ THROUGH THE PASSAGE SLOWLY.

What is one word or phrase that stands out to you?

PAUSE & PRAY

In silence, meditate on this word or phrase.

LECTIO 2: READ THROUGH THE PASSAGE A SECOND TIME.

This time, pray through the passage, reading phrase by phrase.
Talk to God, pausing to listen and respond to Him as you read.

PAUSE & PRAY

In silence, bring your attention to the present moment.

LECTIO 3: READ THROUGH THE PASSAGE A THIRD TIME.

Sit in stillness again as you contemplate the word or phrase that
stood out to you and how it may apply to your life right now.

NOTICE

Notice your body: What are you feeling right now?
Notice your thoughts: What are you thinking right now?
Notice your circumstances: What is happening in your life
right now?

Compassionately consider these things, and listen to what the
Holy Spirit may be revealing to you in light of today's reading and
meditation. What invitation might God be extending to you today?

God is inviting me to . . .

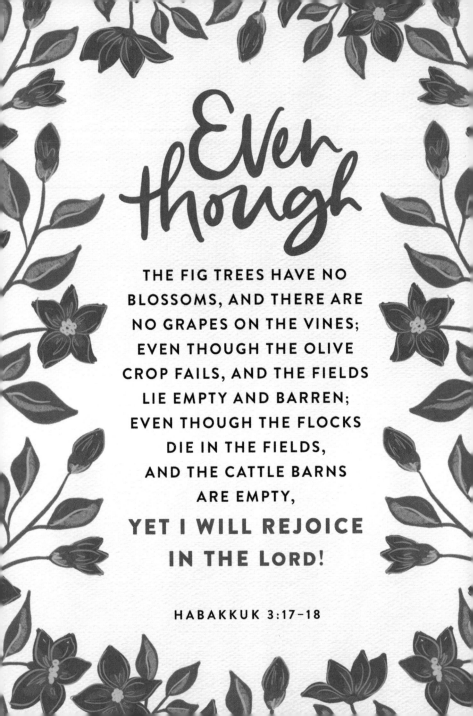

Even though

THE FIG TREES HAVE NO
BLOSSOMS, AND THERE ARE
NO GRAPES ON THE VINES;
EVEN THOUGH THE OLIVE
CROP FAILS, AND THE FIELDS
LIE EMPTY AND BARREN;
EVEN THOUGH THE FLOCKS
DIE IN THE FIELDS,
AND THE CATTLE BARNS
ARE EMPTY,
YET I WILL REJOICE
IN THE LORD!

HABAKKUK 3:17–18

Surrendering Prayer

As I prepare to enter into the rest of my day, Lord,

May my pace be slow and unhurried,
ever aware of Your presence with me.

May my mind be attentive and clear,
noticing the gift of every moment.

May my heart be gentle and kind,
showing compassion to myself and others.

Even if I fail or fall or just fall apart;
even if plans go awry or hopes are dashed;
even if I lose what I love—or whom I love;
even if the worst happens,
may I still trust You, still rejoice in You.

Today, I set aside my expectations for today,
and I accept whatever You give.

Keep turning my thoughts to whatever is worthy of praise.
Transform me to be more like You.

Amen.

Embody

Continue to contemplate the word and invitation God gave you today.

Consider: What is your "even though" today? What's the struggle, the disappointment, the hard thing that makes it difficult to find joy?

30

PRAISE GOD FOR ALL THAT IS TO COME

REVELATION 21:3-7

In Revelation, we find the ultimate message of hope—that now is not the end of the story and there will be a day when all things will be made new, with Jesus' return and God's ultimate plan to usher in a new heaven and new earth. We see a vision of the new Jerusalem coming down within a renewed creation. We see God not abandoning this world but transforming it into something new. We see Jesus sitting not in some far-off, unreachable heaven but making His eternal home among His people, present with us forever and ever. We see Him destroying death and sin once and for all, wiping away every tear and removing sorrow and pain and suffering forever.[27]

It's a future too glorious to adequately imagine, a hope almost too beautiful to believe. But God always keeps His promises; He does what He says He will do. It is with this assurance that we hold to hope and praise God for an eternal ending to our story that is too wonderful for words.

Silence

Begin with a time of silence.

Still your body. . . . Slow your breathing. . . . Quiet your mind.

Focus on being fully present in this moment,
right here, right now.

He will wipe
every tear from
their eyes, and
there will be
no more death
or sorrow or
crying or pain.
All these things
are gone
forever.

REVELATION 21:4

I heard a loud shout from the throne, saying, "Look, God's home is now among his people! He will live with them, and they will be his people. God himself will be with them. He will wipe every tear from their eyes, and there will be no more death or sorrow or crying or pain. All these things are gone forever."

And the one sitting on the throne said, "Look, I am making everything new! . . . To all who are thirsty I will give freely from the springs of the water of life. All who are victorious will inherit all these blessings, and I will be their God, and they will be my children."

REVELATION 21:3–7

Opening Prayer

Everlasting God of all,

This life can be so hard and heavy,
but the struggles of today are never the end
*   of the story.*
Relieve the weight of the burdens I bear,
and fill me with Your weightless grace.

I invite You to speak to me,
to search my heart and shape my life.
Show me what is worthy of praise.

Open my eyes to see You.
Open my ears to hear Your voice.
Open my heart to receive Your Word.
Open my hands to accept whatever
*   You give.*

Draw close to me, Lord,
as I draw close to You.

Amen.

Read & Meditate

Read through the Bible passage three times, taking time to pause and pray and quietly listen to the Holy Spirit speaking to your heart.

LECTIO 1: READ THROUGH THE PASSAGE SLOWLY.
What is one word or phrase that stands out to you?

> **PAUSE & PRAY**
> In silence, meditate on this word or phrase.

LECTIO 2: READ THROUGH THE PASSAGE A SECOND TIME.
This time, pray through the passage, reading phrase by phrase.
Talk to God, pausing to listen and respond to Him as you read.

> **PAUSE & PRAY**
> In silence, bring your attention to the present moment.

LECTIO 3: READ THROUGH THE PASSAGE A THIRD TIME.
Sit in stillness again as you contemplate the word or phrase that
stood out to you and how it may apply to your life right now.

> **NOTICE**
> Notice your body: What are you feeling right now?
> Notice your thoughts: What are you thinking right now?
> Notice your circumstances: What is happening in your life
> right now?

Compassionately consider these things, and listen to what the
Holy Spirit may be revealing to you in light of today's reading and
meditation. What invitation might God be extending to you today?

God is inviting me to . . .

Surrendering Prayer

As I prepare to enter into the rest of my day, Lord,

May my pace be slow and unhurried,
ever aware of Your presence with me.

May my mind be attentive and clear,
noticing the gift of every moment.

May my heart be gentle and kind,
showing compassion to myself and others.

Help me to remember that this is not the end of the story,
that present trials pale in the light of eternity,
that so much glory and beauty and peace are ahead.
You'll wipe away every tear and remove every pain.
You will make everything new.

Today, may I simply find peace and rest in that glorious hope.
And may Your will be done here on earth as it is in heaven.

Keep turning my mind to whatever is worthy of praise.
Continue to transform me to be more like You.

Amen.

Embody

Continue to contemplate the word and invitation God gave you today.

Consider: What is a promise of God that you can hold on to today?

....

....

APPENDIX
Mindfulness Exercises

As you attempt to be still and meditate, your mind will inevitably begin to wander. This is *completely normal*. Your thoughts may be scattered or you may feel some anxiety, but don't let that frustrate or discourage you. Instead, learn to be kind to your wandering mind. If you find yourself struggling to focus because of anxiety, distractions, or racing thoughts, try these simple mindfulness exercises to help you ground yourself in the present moment, calm your anxiety, and process your thoughts with compassion and grace.

BREATH PRAYER

Breath prayer is a simple way to calm your body and mind as you focus your thoughts on the presence of God and the truth in His Word. To practice breath prayer, slow your breathing and repeat a simple phrase or prayer to the rhythm of your inhales and exhales. Here's an example that may help when entering into a time of meditation.

> Inhale: Be still, my soul.
> Exhale: The Lord is with me.

Repeat the breath prayer as you slow your breathing and focus your mind. If your mind wanders, keep gently turning and returning your focus to your breathing and to the breath prayer.

Some other breath prayers to try:

From Isaiah 26:3
> Inhale: Keep me in perfect peace
> Exhale: as I keep my thoughts on You.

From Psalm 119:11
    Inhale: Fill my heart
    Exhale: with Your Word.

From 1 Peter 5:7
    Inhale: I give You my worries and cares,
    Exhale: for You care about me.

From Psalm 130:5
    Inhale: I wait for you, Lord;
    Exhale: my hope is in your Word.[28]

TRAINS OF THOUGHT

Visualize your mind as a train station and your thoughts as trains that pass through. You are sitting at the train station as an observer. You're just watching the trains go by.

Some trains may be new, while others may be frequent travelers through your station. Some move by fast, while others tend to linger for a while.

Right now, you are simply observing your trains of thoughts. You're not making any judgments about them. You're not going to climb aboard any of them or explore the cargo they're carrying. You're simply noticing them and then letting them pass by. You can even say to yourself, "I notice I'm thinking about _____." Then gently guide your focus to the present moment. It may be helpful to bring your attention to your breath, focusing on your inhales and exhales. You can also turn your attention to God's presence with you, visualizing Him sitting right next to you in the train station of your mind.

Do not react to or judge any thoughts that pop up. Simply notice their presence. Then compassionately shift your focus back to the present moment and the presence of God with you in this moment.

Try sitting in silence for three to five minutes, intentionally watching your thoughts pass in and out of your mind.

The goal here is not to empty your mind of thoughts but to simply learn how to observe and notice your thoughts so you can change the way you respond to them. Over time, this practice will help you to be less reactionary and more intentional about the thought trains you choose to board and spend time on. For example, instead of mindlessly riding an anxious train of thought that leads you to fear and worry, you can mindfully notice that thought with nonjudgmental compassion toward yourself and then intentionally shift your focus and turn your attention to what is true (and right and pure and lovely, and so on).

NOTES

1. Nadia Whitehead, "People Would Rather Be Electrically Shocked Than Left Alone with Their Thoughts," *Science*, July 3, 2014, www.science.org.

2. Julene Reese, "New Study Shows Impact of Technology on Relationships," *Utah State Today*, November 18, 2019, www.usu.edu/today/story; Arthur C. Brooks, "Technology Can Make Your Relationships Shallower," *Atlantic*, September 29, 2022, www.theatlantic.com.

3. Jennifer Tucker, *Breath As Prayer* (Nashville: Thomas Nelson, 2022), 27.

4. J. I. Packer, *Knowing God*, IVP Signature Collection ed. (Downers Grove, IL: InterVarsity Press, 2021), loc. 319 of 6384, Kindle.

5. Irene Kraegel, *The Mindful Christian* (Minneapolis: Fortress Press, 2020), 33.

6. Matthew Thorpe and Rachael Ajmera, "12 Science-Based Benefits of Meditation," *Healthline*, www .healthline.com; "Meditation: A Simple, Fast Way to Reduce Stress," *Mayo Clinic*, December 14, 2023, www.mayoclinic.org; David Schechter, "Physical Pain, Emotions, and the Brain," *Mindworks*, https://mindworks.org/blog; "Meditation Research: What Does Science Tell Us About Meditation," *Mindworks*, mindworks.org/blog.

7. Benedict of Nursia, in the prologue to *The Rule of Saint Benedict*, ed. Timothy Fry (Collegeville, MN: Liturgical Press, 1981).

8. Guigo II, quoted in Simon Tugwell, *Ways of Imperfection* (Springfield, IL: Templegate, 1985), 94.

9. Henri J. M. Nouwen, *The Way of the Heart* (San Francisco: HarperSanFrancisco, 1991), 25.

10. Eugene Peterson, *Eat This Book* (Grand Rapids, MI: Wm. B. Eerdmans, 2006), 59.

11. Merriam-Webster, s.v. "truth," www.merriam-webster.com/dictionary/truth.

12. Merriam-Webster, s.v. "honorable," www.merriam-webster.com/dictionary/honorable.

13. Gary M. Burge and Andrew E. Hill, eds., *The Baker Illustrated Bible Commentary* (Grand Rapids, MI: Baker, 2012), loc. 43859 of 46456, Kindle.

14. Merriam-Webster, s.v. "right," www.merriam-webster.com/dictionary/right.

15. Burge and Hill, *Baker Illustrated Bible Commentary*, loc. 18752 of 46456, Kindle.

16. Janet Erskine Stuart, quoted in Elisabeth Elliot, *Suffering Is Never for Nothing* (Nashville: B&H Publishing Group), 14.

17. Merriam-Webster, s.v. "pure," www.merriam-webster.com/dictionary/pure.

18. Burge and Hill, *Baker Illustrated Bible Commentary*, loc. 15277 of 46456, Kindle.

19. Merriam-Webster, s.v. "lovely," www.merriam-webster.com/dictionary/lovely.

20. Peter T. O'Brien, *The Epistle to the Philippians*, (Grand Rapids, MI: Wm. B. Eerdmans, 1991), 505.

21. Burge and Hill, *Baker Illustrated Bible Commentary*, loc. 14764 of 46456, Kindle.

22. Oxford Languages, s.v. "admirable," www.google.com/search?q=admirable+meaning.

23. Merriam-Webster, s.v. "admirable," www.merriam-webster.com/dictionary/admirable.

24. Cambridge Advanced Learner's Dictionary & Thesaurus, s.v. "admirable," https://dictionary.cambridge .org/us/dictionary/english/admirable.

25. Random House Unabridged Dictionary, s.v. "excellent," https://www.dictionary.com/browse/excellent.

26. Joel LeMon, "Commentary on Psalm 66:8–20," *Working Preacher*, May 14, 2023, www.working preacher.org/commentaries/revised-common-lectionary/sixth-sunday-of-easter /commentary-on-psalm-668-20-5.

27. Burge and Hill, *Baker Illustrated Bible Commentary*, loc. 46144-46175 of 46456, Kindle.

28. Tucker, *Breath as Prayer*: 53, 121, 173, 201.

ABOUT THE AUTHOR

Jennifer Tucker is an illustrator, lettering artist, graphic designer, and bestselling author of *Breath as Prayer*. Her work has been featured in multiple publications, including *The Message Canvas Bible*, *New Mercies I See*, and the bestselling coloring book *Whatever Is Lovely*. She lives in central Georgia with her husband, Mark, and two daughters, Emma and Lilly. Jennifer is a devoted follower of Jesus and an advocate for mental health, breath work, and prayer. She writes and shares her art online at littlehousestudio.net.

f @TheLittleHouseStudio

○ @jenn_littlehousestudio